PENGUIN PASSNOTES

An Inspector Calls

Vivian Summers was educated at the Universities of Exeter
and Cambridge. He was head of the English department at
Queen Elizabeth School, Crediton, for over thirty years. He
has also lectured at a college of education and at the
International Summer Schools held at Exeter University.
He is currently an examiner, a lecturer and a freelance writer
and has published several books on English.

PENGUIN PASSNOTES

J. B. PRIESTLEY

An Inspector Calls

VIVIAN SUMMERS
ADVISORY EDITOR: STEPHEN COOTE, M.A., PH.D.

PENGUIN BOOKS

Penguin Books Ltd, Harmondsworth, Middlesex, England
Viking Penguin Inc., 40 West 23rd Street, New York, New York 10010, U.S.A.
Penguin Books Australia Ltd, Ringwood, Victoria, Australia
Penguin Books Canada Limited, 2801 John Street, Markham, Ontario, Canada L3R 1B4
Penguin Books (N.Z.) Ltd, 182–190 Wairau Road, Auckland 10, New Zealand

First published 1987
Copyright © Vivian Summers, 1987
All rights reserved

Extracts from *An Inspector Calls* by J. B. Priestley
are reproduced by kind permission of William
Heinemann Ltd, Publishers, and A. D. Peters & Co.
Ltd, the agents acting on behalf of the author's
estate.

Made and printed in Great Britain by
Richard Clay Ltd, Bungay, Suffolk
Filmset in Monophoto Ehrhardt

Except in the United States of America, this book is sold subject
to the condition that it shall not, by way of trade or otherwise, be lent,
re-sold, hired out, or otherwise circulated without the
publisher's prior consent in any form of binding or cover other than
that in which it is published and without a similar condition
including this condition being imposed on the subsequent purchaser

Examination questions reproduced by permission of the South Western
Examinations Board and the Welsh Joint Education Committee.

Contents

To the Student 7

Introduction: The Life, Works and Thought of
  J. B. Priestley 9

Background to *An Inspector Calls* 14

Synopsis 15

Act by Act Analysis 24

Characters 40

Commentary 60

Glossary 74

Discussion Topics and Examination Questions 76

To the Student

This book is designed to help you with your O-level, CSE or GCSE English Literature examinations. It contains a synopsis of the play, a glossary of the more unfamiliar words and phrases, and a commentary on some of the issues raised by the text. An account of the writer's life is also included for background.

Page references in parentheses refer to the Penguin edition of *Time and the Conways and Other Plays*.

When you use this book, remember that it is no more than an aid to your study. It will help you find passages quickly and perhaps give you some ideas for essays. But remember also: *This book is not a substitute for reading the play, and it is your knowledge and your response that matter*. These are the things that the examiners are looking for, and they are also the things that will give you the most pleasure. Show your knowledge and appreciation to the examiner, and show them clearly.

Introduction: The Life, Works and Thought of J. B. Priestley

John Boynton Priestley was born on 13 September 1894 in Bradford. His grandfather was a mill worker who struggled to send his son, the playwright's father, to London to train as a school teacher. Priestley's mother died soon after his birth, but his father married again, and it was fortunate that his second wife was a kind and loving woman who created a happy home for her husband and stepson. His father was a great influence on the boy, who was deeply attached to him. J. B. Priestley wrote later of him as 'the man socialists have in mind when they write about socialism'. Above all, his father was devoted to the idea of Education, and the writer grew up in a household where teaching was the main topic of conversation. When he announced that he wanted to leave school at sixteen and start work without going on to further education, he was surprised that his father made no objection but found an opening for him in the wool business, of which Bradford was an important centre.

Although books were cherished in the household, there was no literary background to account for J. B. Priestley's emergence as a writer, but he himself had no doubt that this was what he wanted to be. He accepted the idea of working as a clerk in a wool firm because he realized that he needed time to gain experience as a writer and to find his way in the world. He rejected the idea of trying for a job on a newspaper, because even at the age of sixteen he felt that that kind of writing was not for him.

What writing he did had to be crammed into evenings and week-ends, for he was kept at the office until six or seven o'clock at night. But he enjoyed life to the full, going to the theatre and concerts (Bradford had a lively cultural life), walking with friends on the moors, even travelling abroad cheaply as far afield as Denmark and Sweden. These few years just before the First World War had a profound effect on him as he moved among the mill workers, merchants and businessmen of this great Northern city. He wrote in his reminiscences, *Margin Released* (1962), that although he had never lived in Bradford since those early days, 'I still belong at heart to the pre-1914 North Country. Part of me is still in Bradford, can never leave it . . .'

The outbreak of war in 1914 changed everything. The old life in Bradford was to be lost for ever – and with it J. B. Priestley's youthful ambition to own a small cottage on the moors where he could write to his heart's content. Instead he joined the army and served in the Duke of Wellington's and the Devon Regiments, seeing action in France, where he was wounded. In the summer of 1918 he suffered in a gas attack, and this led to his discharge from the army early in 1919 just after the war had ended.

An ex-service grant enabled him to go to Cambridge University, where he took his degree in 1921. After this he had to think of a career, especially as he was now married. He refused offers of academic posts, preferring to try his luck as a writer in London. Here he spent eight years building up a career for himself as a reviewer, essayist and writer of articles. He also obtained regular work as a publisher's reader – advising on manuscripts submitted for publication – and became acquainted with other famous writers such as Bernard Shaw, H. G. Wells, Arnold Bennett and James Barrie.

By the time he was thirty he had had five books published, and in the next three years no less than nine followed. This was typical of his output. Books, plays and novels poured from his pen. His first novel was written in 1927 and was moderately successful, but it was his fourth novel, *The Good Companions* (1929), that really made his name. The story of how a young woman of independent means sets out to travel around the cathedrals of England but instead finds herself running a broken-down concert party (which she renames The Good Companions) had an enormous popular success. This was followed by *Angel Pavement* in 1931.

J. B. Priestley was now regarded as one of England's leading authors. Many other novels followed during his long career, including *The Doomsday Men, Let the People Sing, Bright Day* and *Festival at Farbridge.* Yet despite this array of successful novels, Priestley preferred later in his career to regard himself as primarily a dramatist.

He did not write his first play until 1932. This was *Dangerous*

Corner. It has a link with *An Inspector Calls*, written many years later, in that both deal with a shift in the normal time-scale. Priestley was intrigued by the theories of time expounded by J. W. Dunne in his book, *An Experiment with Time*, and he saw the dramatic possibilities of showing in a play what alternatives time was offering to the characters, unknown to them. In *Dangerous Corner*, the opening pages of the play are performed twice – once at the beginning, when a dangerous corner in the conversation is turned in such a way as to lead to catastrophe, and then again at the end of the play when the corner is turned safely and life goes on as usual. In *An Inspector Calls*, the last lines of the play suggest that the action is to take place all over again – but with a difference. The most famous 'Time' plays of J. B. Priestley are *Time and the Conways* and *I Have Been Here Before*, both written in 1937. In the former play, Priestley uses the amazingly simple device of moving all the characters on several years in the second act and then bringing them back to the present in the last act. In this way we can see how tragically the bright hopes of the Conway family in Act One have been blighted by the passing of time in Act Two. Then when we see them in Act Three we know how poignantly different their future is to be from what they are expecting.

In complete contrast, 1938 saw the production of his farcical comedy, *When We Are Married*, a play which concerns the dilemma of three highly respected couples who, when celebrating their silver weddings, discover they have never been married at all! This was the play chosen to re-open the Whitehall Theatre in London in 1986, and it again proved an enormous success.

With such plays, J. B. Priestley established himself as a major figure in the West End theatre of the 1930s. The coming of the Second World War in 1939 brought Priestley a different kind of fame. Between June and October 1940 he broadcast a series of Postscripts to the BBC's Sunday night nine o'clock news bulletins that seemed to listeners to be the true voice of Britain in those difficult days after the retreat from Dunkirk. Speaking of simple things that ordinary people cherished, he made them appear important and worth fighting for and his effect on the morale of the nation was immense. So famous were his broadcasts that it surprises people to learn that they lasted only a few months, although he continued to broadcast overseas three or four times a week. He also wrote novels and plays reflecting the country at war and voicing hopes of a better future.

In the post-war years Priestley continued to be very active as a writer. In 1946 no less than three new plays were produced, one of which was *An Inspector Calls.* A year later he wrote *The Linden Tree,* one of his most admired plays, which an eminent critic described as 'the best domestic play of our time'. After this his interest in writing for the theatre gradually declined, although in 1952 he wrote in collaboration with his third wife, Jacquetta Hawkes, an experimental piece called *Dragon's Mouth,* and two more plays followed in the 1950s. In his later years his writing mostly took the form of essays, reminiscences, social history and literary criticism, including the wide-ranging survey, *Literature and Western Man* (1960).

No student of *An Inspector Calls* can be unaware of the author's burning sense of the need for social justice. The play lashes the selfishness of the well-to-do classes who use other people for their own profit and pleasure, and promises destruction if they do not change their ways. Priestley inherited from his father a belief in socialism. What he saw in Bradford, with its rich factory owners and impoverished mill workers, reinforced his views. In *Margin Released* (1962) he recalls the managers who would refuse mill girls an extra shilling a week but 'could be found in distant pubs turning the prettiest and weakest of them into tarts', and he goes on to say how he made use of this in *An Inspector Calls.* But his socialism was never fanatical; his whole temperament was too mature for that. He once summed up his views quite simply as being 'for the poor and against the rich'. He never became a member of the Labour Party, although he campaigned vigorously for it in the General Election of 1945, believing that Britain needed a socialist government to lead it into post-war reconstruction. He even stood for Parliament as an Independent for Cambridge University (at that time some universities had their own M Ps) and, although defeated, polled more votes than any other progressive candidate had ever done in that constituency.

He once wrote that it was misleading to call him a socialist. He believed that the most important thing was the freedom of the individual and he saw the tyranny both of Communism and Big Business as being the enemy of this. The task of government, as he saw it, was to protect the individual. His concern, as in *An Inspector Calls,* was for the unfortunate Eva Smith and the 'millions and millions and millions of Eva Smiths and John Smiths still left with us, with their lives, their hopes and fears, their suffering, and chance of happiness . . .'

Although not a committee-man by nature, J. B. Priestley did serve on a number of public bodies, notably as UK delegate to conferences of UNESCO and on various theatre boards. He was given many honours, including doctorates from the universities of Birmingham, Bradford and St Andrew's. It was most appropriate that he should have been made an Honorary Freeman of the City of Bradford in 1973. He received his highest honour in 1977 when the Queen made him a member of the Order of Merit. He died in 1984 at the age of eighty-nine.

Background to An Inspector Calls

'I wrote this play at top speed, finishing it within a week.' This was J. B. Priestley's own account of the composition of *An Inspector Calls*. Remarkable as this seems, it was not unusual for Priestley to produce substantial work in a very short time. It has been said that when he wrote slowly and laboriously he produced inferior work, whereas his best efforts always came in a very quick spate of writing. The explanation must be that his best ideas germinated and grew in his mind to the point that when he began to write he knew exactly what he wanted to say and could get it on to the paper with the utmost speed. Moreover, he was one of the most prolific writers and words came very easily to him.

It is surprising that this play about a very English family was first produced in Moscow in the summer of 1945, just as the war ended. J. B. Priestley was on a three-month visit to Russia – a rare honour for an English writer in those days – and he travelled widely in that country where his books were very well known. The Russians hailed him as a great man of letters. His views were sufficiently socialist to be politically acceptable to them and they chose to ignore the attacks he had made on Communism. His new play was performed simultaneously in two Moscow theatres. It was a great success and was soon to be seen in New York, Paris and other European capitals.

It was first produced in London in 1946 at the New Theatre. The part of the Inspector was played by Ralph Richardson, and Eric Birling was played by Alec Guinness – two actors destined to be knighted for their services to the English theatre. Since its first production the play has been performed innumerable times all over the world on stage and television. A film was made of it in 1953, with Alistair Sim as the Inspector. In recent years it has been among the texts most frequently set for English Literature examinations.

Synopsis

ACT ONE

It is a spring evening in 1912. At the home of the Birling family, an engagement dinner is taking place. Sheila, the daughter of the prosperous manufacturer Arthur Birling, is to marry Gerald Croft, son of a rival manufacturer, Sir George Croft. The forthcoming marriage may lead to a time when the two family firms cease to be competitors. Despite the convivial atmosphere, there is just a hint that all is not well between the young couple when Sheila refers to the way Gerald lost touch with her the previous summer. Sheila's brother, Eric, is slightly drunk and this adds to the feeling of unease. However, toasts are drunk and Gerald presents Sheila with an engagement ring. Then Mr Birling insists on making a speech. In it he expresses his pleasure at the engagement and assures the couple that they are marrying at a good time: prosperity for employers like himself is increasing, there is less threat of labour troubles and he does not believe there will be a war with Germany. Speaking 'as a hardheaded, practical man of business', he sees material progress in the world making wars impossible. He foresees war scares and capital versus labour problems being quite forgotten by the time the children of Gerald and Sheila will be thinking of marriage – say in 1940!

Mrs Birling leaves the room with Sheila and Eric and so Birling is alone with his future son-in-law. Birling mentions confidentially that he senses that Gerald's mother, Lady Croft, feels that her son might have married into a family socially superior to the Birlings, but he goes on to assure Gerald that he is very likely to receive a knighthood in the next Honours list. He adds laughingly that there should be no obstacle to this, providing he keeps out of the police court and avoids any scandal.

Eric returns to join the other men over their port. He has left his mother and sister discussing clothes. When his father explains how clothes are important to a woman's self-respect, Eric seems on the point of letting slip a remark about his personal experience of this, but checks himself at once. Mr Birling is amused that Eric may have been up to something, young men having more time and money to spend than he did in his youth. He goes on more seriously to give Gerald and Eric his basic philosophy: a man must look after himself and his family and not bother about new-fangled ideas which say we should all look after everyone else in the community, for 'a man has to mind his own business and look after himself and his own . . .'

At this moment the door bell rings. Edna, the maid, announces that an Inspector has called. Birling and Gerald are quite relaxed about this, but Eric becomes distinctly uneasy. The visitor who enters is an Inspector Goole. Birling, who knows all the local police, does not recognize him and suggests he has been recently transferred to the town. The Inspector agrees. He says he has come for information about a girl who has just died in the infirmary after swallowing strong disinfectant – a case of suicide. Birling cannot understand why he is being asked about her, but the Inspector reveals that a letter and a diary were found in the girl's room. It seems that she once worked in Birling's factory. Her name was Eva Smith and the Inspector has a photograph of her. He shows it to Birling but refuses to let the other men see it.

Birling recognizes the girl and recalls that two years earlier she was a ringleader of a strike for higher pay. The strike failed and he sacked her. The Inspector exasperates him by asking why he dismissed her. He replies that it is his duty to keep down labour costs. Gerald supports him, but Eric takes the opposite view, much to his father's annoyance. Birling asks what happened to the girl after she left his employment: did she get into trouble or go on the streets? The Inspector's reply suggests that more of the story will unfold.

Unaware that an Inspector has called, Sheila enters the room. She asks why the men have not joined the ladies in the drawing-room. Believing that the matter cannot concern Sheila, Mr Birling tries to send her from the room, but the Inspector stops her and tells her about the girl's death. Sheila is shocked by the story. Gerald feels that the inquiry is getting nowhere, and that as the girl died long after leaving Birling's factory they can have nothing more to contribute since they know nothing about her after that. The Inspector startles them all by saying, 'Are you sure you don't know?' Sheila voices their feelings: 'You talk as if we were responsible . . .'

The Inspector outlines the next stage in the girl's story: she was unemployed for two months and stopped calling herself Eva Smith. Half-starved and almost friendless, she was cheap labour but was lucky enough to get a job in Milwards, the fashion shop patronized by Sheila herself. She enjoyed the work but was dismissed after only two months because a customer complained about her. Sheila becomes agitated on hearing this and questions the Inspector closely about the girl. He shows her the photograph; very distressed, she runs from the room. Birling goes off to question her further and also to tell Mrs Birling what is happening.

The Inspector refuses to let Gerald see the photograph, but says he will have an opportunity to speak in due course. Eric is not allowed to leave the room. Sheila returns and says to the Inspector, 'You knew it was me all the time, didn't you?' She has admitted to her father that she was the customer who caused the girl to be sacked, but the Inspector does not agree that she was the one entirely responsible for the girl's tragedy. Both she and her father were partly to blame. When Eric asks what she did, she explains how she tried on something at Milwards which did not suit her; the dead girl had previously held up the garment in front of herself and it suited her admirably. Moreover she was very pretty. When Sheila tried the garment on, she caught the girl smiling at the sales assistant as if to say the customer looked awful in it. This made Sheila so angry that she insisted the girl be dismissed; otherwise she and her mother would withdraw their custom from the shop. She admitted that she was jealous because the girl was so pretty.

Full of remorse, Sheila cries, 'Oh – why had this to happen?' The Inspector says that is why he has come – to know why it happened. He is not going until he knows *all* that happened. He adds that the girl changed her name to Daisy Renton. Gerald reacts to this and agitatedly pours himself a drink. Eric takes the Inspector to see his father in the next room, leaving Sheila and Gerald alone together.

At once Sheila asks Gerald how he knew Eva Smith – or Daisy Renton – since it is obvious that the name meant something to him. Gerald admits he knew the girl but is unwilling to say more. Sheila continues to question him, and from his silence has confirmation of her suspicions: he was seeing this girl last spring and summer when he was neglecting her. Gerald finally admits it and apologizes, but as it was all over six months before, he does not think it affects the suicide and he asks Sheila not to tell the Inspector. But Sheila senses that the Inspector already knows – and much more besides. 'You'll see, you'll see,' she cries. The door opens and the Inspector enters. 'Well?' he asks.

ACT TWO

Looking at Gerald, he repeats the question, 'Well?' Realizing that he is going to be questioned, Gerald tries to persuade Sheila to leave the room, but she refuses. He thinks she is eager to see him 'put through it', just as she herself has been, and a quarrel springs up between them. The Inspector intervenes to explain that it is important for Sheila to stay and hear Gerald's story; otherwise she will feel that she alone caused the girl's death.

Before Gerald can say any more, Mrs Birling enters the room full of self-confidence and quite unaware that her manner is completely out of keeping with what has happened. She tries to converse with the Inspector in her best social manner, to the horror of Sheila, who cannot stand the falseness of it. She appeals to her mother, for her own sake, not to make matters worse by pretending the family know nothing about the dead girl. Sheila already realizes that the Inspector is a very special person who will break down any sham. Mrs Birling does not heed the warning and blunders on, even to the extent of warning the Inspector that her husband is an ex-Lord Mayor and that he is still a magistrate.

When the Inspector asks where Mr Birling is, he is told that he is looking after Eric, who has had too much to drink. Mrs Birling is shocked to learn from Sheila and Gerald that Eric has been a heavy drinker for the past two years. Mr Birling returns to the room without Eric. The Inspector says he will see him in due course. Meanwhile he turns his attention back to Gerald. He asks when Gerald first met Daisy Renton. The young man tells him that it was in a bar at the Palace Music Hall. He dropped in there one evening and saw a girl being accosted by the fat and unpleasant Alderman Meggarty. He rescued her from him and took her for a drink and a chat at the

County Hotel. She just wanted to talk and to receive a little friendliness. She told Gerald that she was called Daisy Renton, that her parents were dead, and she made some reference to losing her job after a strike at a factory. She also mentioned a shop but was very vague about what actually happened there. They met again two nights later and, as she was penniless and about to be turned out of her lodgings, Gerald moved her into some rooms he had at his disposal and he also gave her a small allowance. He did this entirely out of sympathy for her, but after a while she did become his mistress.

Sheila asks him whether he was in love with the girl or not. He is unsure but believes that the girl felt more for him than he did for her. Although sharply critical of him, Sheila praises his honesty and admits her own share in the tragedy. The Inspector makes Gerald tell how the affair ended. Apparently he broke it off in the September, giving the girl enough money to live on for the rest of the year. The Inspector supplies the information that she went away for about two months to a seaside place. Her diary referred to her feeling that there would never again be as good a time for her as that which she had spent with Gerald.

The Inspector allows Gerald to go for a short walk, but before he leaves, Sheila returns his engagement ring. She says they are not the same people who sat down to dinner that evening. They must begin to get to know each other all over again.

Sheila remarks that the Inspector never showed Gerald the girl's photo. He does, however, show it to Mrs Birling, insisting that she looks at it. She affects not to recognize the girl, and when she says as much, the Inspector bluntly accuses her of not telling the truth. Mr Birling takes offence at this and demands an apology, but Sheila – as always the one who perceives what is happening – explains that none of them has any excuse for putting on airs. What is more, she believes that her mother's expression revealed that she knew the girl, though Sheila cannot think why. A door slams, suggesting either that Gerald has returned or that Eric has gone out. Mr Birling goes to investigate.

The Inspector begins his examination of Mrs Birling, who, it appears, was the chairman of a meeting of a Women's Charity Organization held two weeks before. Mr Birling returns at this point to report that Eric must have been the person who has just left the house. The Inspector insists that Eric is needed for his inquiries and will have to be sought if he does not return soon. Then the Inspector astonishes Mr Birling and Sheila by putting it to Mrs Birling that she saw Eva Smith more recently than either of them – at that meeting only two weeks previously. Mrs Birling reluctantly admits it, but the girl offended her by calling herself 'Mrs Birling'. At first she claimed she was married and had been deserted by her husband, but under questioning admitted that this was not so. The girl said she called herself 'Mrs Birling' because it was the first name that came into her head. The real Mrs Birling took a dislike to her and used her influence to make the committee refuse assistance. She felt she only did her duty and her conscience was clear. The Inspector, however, tells her that she did a terrible wrong, for the girl was pregnant. Sheila is very upset at what her mother has done, and the assurance from the Inspector that Gerald Croft was not the father does little to calm her.

Mrs Birling, however, is prepared to defend herself: the girl had been caught out telling lies; she also claimed to know who the father of the child was, but would not appeal to him to support her because he was a silly youngster who drank too much and who had – up to then – been stealing in order to give her money. Mrs Birling viewed all this as a pack of lies. The Inspector points out that if the girl's story was true, then she was acting very nobly in trying to keep the young father out of further trouble by seeking money from the Charity Organization. Mrs Birling admits that the girl's death was regrettable but does not accept any blame for it. She places the responsibility on the girl herself and on the father, who should be publicly exposed and dealt with severely. Sheila suddenly realizes the way the evidence is pointing and in alarm cries out to her mother to stop. But Mrs Birling sweeps on in her denunciation of the young man, and she insists that it is the Inspector's duty to find him and show him up publicly. The Inspector agrees and says that for that reason, in order to do his duty, he will stay in their home and wait. At this, the truth dawns on Mrs Birling and on her husband also and they are terrified. The house door is heard to open and close. They all wait for the door of the dining-room to open. When it does so, the pale and distressed figure who enters is – Eric.

ACT THREE

Eric realizes that they all know his part in the affair. His parents and sister briefly exchange recriminations with him and each other, but the Inspector cuts across them with the demand to hear Eric's story without interruption. In answer to the Inspector's questions, Eric tells how he first met the girl in November at the Palace bar. He got rather drunk, and the girl was not entirely sober either as she had been drinking on an empty stomach. He insisted on going home to her lodgings, and although she was reluctant to let him in, she finally did so as in his condition he might have become troublesome. It was then that they made love, although he has no recollection of it now.

Mrs Birling is very distressed at this story and Sheila is asked to take her from the room. Eric goes on to tell how he met the girl on other evenings and went home with her. On one such occasion she told him she was to have a baby. Both were very worried about it, but the girl refused to marry him because she said he did not love her. Eric insisted on giving her money until she refused to accept any more. By then he had given her fifty pounds.

When his father demands to know where he got the money from, Eric admits that he took it from the office of his father's firm where he worked. At this point Sheila and Mrs Birling return to the room. Mr Birling bitterly tells them that his son has admitted being the father of the child and also to stealing money. When he asks why Eric did not come to him for money and help, his son tells him: '. . . you're not the kind of father a chap could go to when he's in trouble . . .'

The Inspector asks him to confirm that the girl would take no more money from him once she knew it was stolen. When Eric asks how the fact was known, Sheila reveals that the girl told their mother. Eric asks how this happened and the Inspector tells him how his mother and her committee refused to help her. Eric, near breaking point, curses his mother for killing the girl and her own grandchild. Mrs Birling's distressed excuse – 'I didn't understand' – is brusquely dismissed by Eric's retort, 'You don't understand anything. You never did . . .'

At this point the Inspector intervenes to deliver his summing-up. He reminds them all of their part in the girl's tragedy, and goes on to tell them of the millions and millions of Eva Smiths and John Smiths in the world whose lives are intertwined with ours: 'We are responsible for one another.'

The Inspector departs and Mr and Mrs Birling turn on Eric. His father is furious that all this is likely to become a public scandal and ruin his chances of a knighthood. Sheila is appalled that her parents seem to have learnt nothing from the Inspector's visit but are still only concerned about their own selfish interests. She also notes that the Inspector arrived immediately after her father declared that a man has to look after himself and take no notice of cranks who tell us everybody has to look after everybody else. The coincidence seems significant: was he *really* a police inspector? Mr Birling agrees that the officer did not behave like an ordinary police inspector. He blames the children for allowing the Inspector to make them admit so much. He believes that the Inspector, possessing only minimal information, bluffed them into confessing everything. He tries to think out a course of action, but there is a ring at the front door. Gerald has returned from his walk, bringing important news: he has just met a police sergeant of his acquaintance and asked him if he knew an Inspector Goole. The sergeant assured him that no such inspector belonged to their force. Mr Birling rings up the Chief Constable and receives the same information.

To Mr and Mrs Birling and Gerald this makes all the difference: the man must be an impostor and a hoaxer. The important thing now is for them all to keep their heads and avoid a public scandal. But Eric and Sheila are shocked at this attitude. For them, the fate of Eva Smith is all that matters and each of them contributed to it. But Gerald has had another surprising thought: they have all admitted having dealings with the girl – but how do they know it is the *same girl*? They go over the investigation by the Inspector and realize that he never showed the photograph to more than one person at a time and so he may have been using different pictures. He trapped Mrs Birling into admitting she had seen Eva Smith, although the girl never used that name before the committee. Neither Gerald nor Eric has been shown any photo at all. With these uncertainties in mind, Mr Birling now makes a further point: since there may have been several girls, not one, can they be sure that *any* girl killed herself? To settle this point, Gerald rings the infirmary. He is assured that no girl has died there that day, no one has been admitted after drinking disinfectant and they have had no suicide for months.

Mr and Mrs Birling and Gerald are highly delighted, thinking that they have been the victims of nothing more than an elaborate hoax. Sheila, although relieved, is far from happy. Even though there has been no suicide, each of the family (and Gerald) has behaved very badly towards a girl. The attempt to pretend that nothing has happened frightens her. Her father dismisses this as nonsense and tells her to ask Gerald for the engagement ring again. But Eric supports his sister; she is horrified that the others appear unwilling to learn any lesson from what has happened. They had begun to learn something but now they have stopped. Mr and Mrs Birling advise their children to go to bed – things will seem different in the morning. Gerald asks Sheila to accept back the engagement ring, but she replies that it is too soon; she must have time to think.

The phone rings and Mr Birling answers it. Panic-stricken, he turns to tell his family that the call was from the police: a girl has died after swallowing some disinfectant – and a police inspector is on his way to ask them some questions . . .

Act by Act Analysis

ACT ONE

The whole action of the play takes place in one room, and the set and furnishings tell us a good deal about the Birlings. 'The general effect is substantial and heavily comfortable,' says the stage direction, 'but not cosy and homelike.' This reflects the life of a household where there is material prosperity but not a united family feeling, despite the superficial happiness of the engagement party.

Mrs Birling is described as being her husband's social superior, and an awareness of social niceties comes out during the opening conversation. Mr Birling, who is a social climber, has bought the same port as is bought by Gerald's father, Sir George Croft. Mrs Birling has to be persuaded to drink some on this special occasion, since it was not usual for ladies to take port with the men. She also gently reproaches her husband for publicly praising the cook: such a thing is 'not done'. In such small ways we are made aware that Mr Birling is not a gentleman and that Mrs Birling is of a better class than her husband. The play has much to do with people's attitudes to others in society and to those of a different social class, and the opening exchanges serve to alert us to this.

The play is hardly a minute old before the first remark is made that suggests that the happiness of this engagement party may not be as complete as it seems. Sheila reminds Gerald that he never came near her all last summer and she wondered what had happened to him. His excuse that he was 'awfully busy at the works' does not sound convincing. Almost immediately after this, Eric guffaws for no apparent reason and Sheila ascribes it to his being 'squiffy'. This harmless exchange foreshadows the revelation much later of Eric's drinking problem.

From these scattered remarks, various tensions and problems are suggested. For the moment, however, these are held in abeyance while Mr Birling speaks of his pleasure at the engagement of his daughter to Gerald Croft. It quickly appears that what pleases Birling especially is that the marriage will lead to cooperation between the firms of Crofts Ltd and Birling and Company, who up to now have been rivals. Crofts is the older and bigger firm, so once again we see Birling's anxiety to improve his material prospects in the world. Significantly he speaks of their working together for 'lower costs and higher prices' – something that would be good for the factory owners but not for the workers or consumers!

Birling proposes a toast to the young couple, and amid the congratulations Eric tipsily tells Gerald, 'She's got a nasty temper sometimes – but she's not bad really' – another hint of something of importance later when we hear how Sheila's quick temper cost Eva Smith her job.

The long after-dinner speech which Birling makes (pp. 165–6) is full of dramatic irony, for J. B. Priestley wrote the play in 1946, well knowing that Birling's confidence that there would be no war was wrong-headed since the First World War would begin only two years after he spoke. His belief that by 1940 all labour troubles and war scares would be a thing of the past would be seen by his audiences as very ironic indeed, for in 1939 came the outbreak of the Second World War, after a decade full of labour problems and marked by the great economic Depression. Mr Birling, in characteristic fashion, believes that material progress – new developments in transport, for example – will make war impossible. As a hard-headed practical man of business, he thinks he knows!

When the ladies and Eric withdraw, Birling mentions confidentially to Gerald the possibility of his receiving a knighthood. He is conscious that Gerald's mother thinks her son is marrying into a socially inferior family, and he has no objection to a hint being dropped to Lady Croft about the honour he hopes to be awarded.

We are getting near the point when the Inspector will call and change all their lives, but J. B. Priestley has another hint to drop and one more attitude to establish before that happens. The hint concerns Eric. In a casual conversation about the importance of clothes to women, he eagerly says, 'Yes, I remember – ' and then checks himself (p. 168). The audience wonders what particular knowledge of women and their clothes he has and why he suddenly refuses to go on. It does of course refer to his liaison with Eva Smith – something that will make an enormous impact when it is revealed much later on.

The attitude to be established is one which is about to be challenged by the events that follow: this is Birling's philosophy that 'a man has to make his own way – has to look after himself . . .' He gives this advice to Gerald and Eric over a glass of port and enlarges on the subject by saying how nowadays cranks talk and write as though everybody had to look after everybody else. He rejects this as nonsense: 'a man has to mind his own business and look after himself and his own . . .' (p. 168). It is when these words are on his lips that – An Inspector Calls.

In this opening section of the play, J. B. Priestley has skilfully introduced the family, established their social positions, and allowed Mr Birling plenty of scope to expound his selfish, materialistic philosophy. He has also planted small hints, of no great importance at the time, of Gerald's missing weeks the previous summer, of Eric's drinking, of Sheila's temper and of the necessity for there to be no scandal in the next few weeks if Mr Birling is to gain his knighthood. The scene is set for the Inspector to enter this self-satisfied family circle and reveal each person's guilty secret so that the scandal Mr Birling dreads seems certain to explode around him. The different effect the Inspector has on the various characters will also be a main topic of the play.

'Please, sir, an inspector's called,' says the maid. Even in the few seconds before the Inspector enters the room there is time for another hint of tension, when Eric reacts sharply to Gerald's joke that the police might be after him. We feel that perhaps Eric *has* been up to something, but when the Inspector is shown in it is Mr Birling that he wants to question. The story of the girl dying in the infirmary seems to have no relevance to anyone present, but when the Inspector shows the photograph of Eva Smith to Birling, he recognizes her as one of his former employees. The Inspector explains his refusal to allow Eric and Gerald to see the photo as simply his policy of dealing with one person and one line of inquiry at a time; but it assumes great importance towards the end of the play when it is realized that by never allowing any two people to look at the picture together, the Inspector may have been showing a different photo to each person.

Since Mr Birling is to be questioned, Gerald politely suggests that he should leave the room, but even this small courtesy turns into something significant when the Inspector, learning that Gerald has just become engaged to Sheila, says he would prefer him to stay. The implication is that he should be aware of what his future father-in-law has been doing. Understandably Birling resents this, saying that something that happened nearly two years ago cannot have anything to do with the girl's suicide that day. But the Inspector speaks of 'a chain of events', and Birling was the first link. When Birling voices the opinion that it would be awkward if we were to be held responsible for everything that happened to everyone we had ever had anything to do with, Eric agrees (surely ironically), reminding him of his advice to the men after dinner. Birling now finds this embarrassing.

When Birling explains how he handled the strike for higher pay led by Eva Smith, he feels he acted sensibly and as a successful business man should. Gerald supports him, but it is noticeable that Eric consistently takes the opposite view. His sympathy for the girl leads to quite an outburst on his part, and he receives a rebuke from his father, who does not see in him someone who will be able to handle employees himself one day (p. 174).

Birling's part in Eva Smith's tragedy has been established and in his view that should be the end of the matter, but Sheila's entrance moves the unfolding story along to its next stage. Gerald is confident that what happened in the next two years is what is really important, and none of them knows anything about that. 'Are you sure you don't know?' asks the Inspector, looking in turn at Gerald, Eric and Sheila (p. 175). It is at this moment of the play that attentive members of the audience will guess that each of the three must know something and that more links in the chain of events will soon emerge.

It is now Sheila's turn. From the first moment she heard of the girl's story she has been deeply moved by it, and as the Inspector supplies details of what happened next she continues to feel compassion: 'But these girls aren't cheap labour – they're *people*' (p. 177). Sheila follows the events sympathetically, but the story of the girl at Milwards who was sacked following a customer's complaint alarms her. A glance at the photograph confirms her fears and she runs from the room. Mr Birling and Gerald are astonished, but to the audience the implication is clear enough. Sheila was the customer.

The characters in the play are so preoccupied with what is being revealed about them that up to this time no one has taken much notice of the way the Inspector talks. Of course Birling has objected to some of his questioning, but it should be noticed that the Inspector does more than simply ask questions: he also comments and in a way that would not be usual for a policeman. For example (p. 172), he surprises Birling by asking why he refused to raise the factory girls' wages, and he supports Eric when he says that there is no freedom for a worker 'if you can't go and work somewhere else' (p. 173). He comments on the same page, '. . . after all it's better to ask for the earth than to take it.' The Inspector's most direct social comments come when he talks of the many young women like Eva Smith who provide the cheap labour for factories and warehouses. He adds, 'In fact, I've thought that it would do us all a bit of good if sometimes we tried to put ourselves in the place of these young women counting their pennies in their dingy little back bedrooms' (p. 177). With such remarks, he makes us feel already that he is somewhat different from an ordinary police inspector.

Sheila's sudden exit from the room makes a dramatic effect, and her return, admitting that she was the customer, makes another one. But J. B. Priestley uses the time she is absent to keep Eric and Gerald in our minds: from the few exchanges between the two young men and the Inspector, we are quite prepared for them to be brought into the story in due course. For the time, though, our interest centres on Sheila, who is very ready to admit her responsibility – and her bad temper (something Eric alluded to in the first moments of the play).

Sheila's remark, 'You knew it was me all the time, didn't you?' (p. 179) is an early example of her awareness that the Inspector has some special way of knowing about people. While the insensitive Mr Birling continues to think of the visitor as a policeman – and later as a hoaxer – Sheila increasingly feels the strange quality of the Inspector and that there is something about him that cannot be explained in human terms.

It should be noted that, although the Inspector leads her on by asking certain questions, it is Sheila herself who admits to being to blame, as when she says miserably, 'So I'm really responsible?' (p. 179) and 'It was my own fault' (p. 180). Of all the members of the family, she is the most ready to express regret and to wish she had acted differently. But the Inspector is at pains to limit her feelings of guilt, because others are equally to blame and the guilt must be shared, just as responsibility for other people in our world should also be shared by all.

The Inspector sums up the story of Eva Smith to the time she left Milwards and then adds the next step: '. . . she changed her name to Daisy Renton –' (p. 181). The end of the act is approaching and J. B. Priestley is now preparing the ground for Act Two. He neatly removes the Inspector and Eric from the room and leaves Sheila alone with Gerald Croft. She has noticed – as we all have – his nervous reaction to the name 'Daisy Renton', and she now takes over the role of the Inspector, asking him bluntly how he came to know the girl. She is impatient of his efforts to avoid admitting that he knew her, and when he reluctantly does so she is scathingly contemptuous of his wish to keep the episode quiet: 'Why – you fool – *he knows*. Of course he knows.' Again Sheila shows that she has sensed that the Inspector has more than ordinary knowledge of these things. Gerald cuts a poor figure as he tries to avoid the inevitable questioning. But he has no chance. The Inspector is in the doorway with his chilling question: 'Well?'

ACT TWO

To begin each subsequent act exactly where the previous one finished is a clever device by J. B. Priestley to maintain tension – or at any rate quickly to restore it after the intervals. At the beginning of Act Two the Inspector repeats his one-word question, and now it is Gerald's turn to reveal his part in the girl's story. Guilt breeds distrust, and this is shown in the quarrel that springs up between Gerald and Sheila. Gerald suggests that Sheila should be spared any further part in the questioning. It sounds as though he is being considerate to her, but beneath this lies his wish to avoid the shame of confessing his affair with Daisy Renton in front of his fiancée. He says he only wishes to spare her something she will hate (p. 183) and he misunderstands her reply: 'It can't be any worse for me than it has been. And it might be better' (p. 184). He takes this to mean that she wants to see him 'put through it', just as she has been – a nasty and spiteful interpretation to put on the remark of someone he is supposed to love. Sheila surely meant to say that it would be better if they both knew the whole truth about the dead girl and who is to blame. The misunderstanding causes a sharp quarrel and foreshadows the breaking of the engagement. The Inspector has to intervene strongly and explain Sheila's position: she knows she is to blame but can't and won't believe that she alone is responsible. The Inspector makes one of his un-police-like pronouncements: 'You see, we have to share something. If there is nothing else, we'll have to share our guilt.' This reinforces Sheila's sense of the strangeness of this officer. She approaches him with wonder, saying, 'I don't understand about you' (p. 184). His reply explains nothing, but they face each other, the Inspector regarding her calmly, she staring 'wonderingly and dubiously'. No words are spoken, but we feel some kind of rapport has been established between the two.

We now expect to hear Gerald's story; but J. B. Priestley is a master of suspense and the play takes an unexpected turn with the intervention of Mrs Birling. Instead of details about Gerald, we find ourselves sharing the embarrassment of Sheila as her mother plays the role of the gracious lady of the house, patronizing the Inspector and trying to deal with him as someone rather inferior with whom she will be polite although naturally quite unable to help him with his inquiries. Sheila is not only embarrassed by this display, but very much aware that her mother will somehow find herself involved as much as everyone else and that the more she puts on airs the worse will be her fall. Mrs Birling's supercilious reference to 'girls of that class', her complaint of the Inspector's 'impertinence' and her reference to her husband having once been Lord Mayor and being still a magistrate show her to be utterly on the wrong wavelength, as she blunders on regardless of the appeals of Sheila (and eventually Gerald) for her to stop (p. 186).

Her descent into reality comes very swiftly. Her excuse for Eric's 'excitable silly mood' – that he is unused to drinking – leads directly to Sheila's revelation that, on the contrary, 'He's been steadily drinking too much for the last two years.' Mrs Birling's complaint that it is Sheila and not the Inspector who is revealing these home-truths is significant: the Inspector rarely accuses directly; he simply puts people in the position where they acknowledge the truth which up to then they have kept hidden. Sheila reinforces this view when her father angrily criticizes the way the Inspector is conducting the case and says to him, 'I don't propose to give you much more rope.' To this Sheila replies, 'No, he's giving us rope – so that we'll hang ourselves' (p. 188).

By this time the self-confidence of this 'respectable' family has been thoroughly shaken. Mr Birling's heartless business methods, Sheila's bad temper, Eric's drinking and Mrs Birling's insensitivity have all been revealed. On the positive side, truth is being faced and – certainly as far as Sheila is concerned – responsibility is being acknowledged for past wrong-doing.

Now Gerald Croft has to declare his part in the tragedy of Eva Smith – or Daisy Renton. In doing so, he has to face the bitterness of his fiancée, who wants to hear the story of the man who deserted the girl he is supposed to be in love with: 'I wouldn't miss it for worlds –' (p. 189).

Gerald is allowed to tell his story at some length and with little interruption. We should note that when he gives Daisy Renton's account of her background, she mentions leaving her job after a strike and 'something about a shop too, but wouldn't say which it was, and she was deliberately vague about what happened' (p. 190). This is important because it allows the characters towards the end of the play to consider the idea that they may not have been dealing with one and the same girl. J. B. Priestley skilfully avoids giving any clinching evidence that each one of them had actually met the one Eva Smith.

The strange power of the Inspector is shown once again in the latter part of Gerald's story, when he carefully explains to the officer his motives in installing the girl in the rooms in Morgan Terrace. '. . . Why are you saying that to him? You ought to be saying it to me,' complains Sheila. When Gerald tries to explain, she does it for him: 'I know. Somehow he makes you' (p. 191).

Gerald pursues his story to the final parting with Daisy Renton, having to endure not only the impersonal questions of the Inspector but also the more emotional questions and reactions of Sheila. She does not give him an easy time with her sharp comments, and Gerald is not surprised when she returns him the engagement ring. But her remarks when she does so are thoughtful and serious: she gives him credit for honesty, for the way he pitied Daisy Renton, and she acknowledges that it was her fault that the girl was so desperate when he met her: '. . . in some odd way, I rather respect you more than I've ever done before.' But she knows that their relationship is now very different from an hour or two before when they sat down to dinner: 'We'd have to start all over again, getting to know each other –' (p. 194). Gerald does not share Mrs Birling's view that 'we've just about come to an end of this wretched business'. Nor do we, the audience.

It is Mrs Birling herself who occupies most of the attention from now on to the end of the act. The quick-witted Sheila has noticed that Gerald was never shown a picture of Daisy Renton – the name alone was enough to make him react nervously. Now Mrs Birling demands to see the photograph and the Inspector shows it to her. She tries to evince no surprise, but the Inspector is certain that she recognizes the girl. He is very severe on her attempt to feign ignorance: 'You're not telling the truth.' This blunt statement contrasts strongly with the artificial manner that has been adopted up to now by Mrs Birling. Her husband's blustering attempts to make the Inspector apologize because Birling is a 'public man' receives the massive rebuke: 'Public men, Mr Birling, have responsibilities as well as privileges' (p. 195). Again it falls to Sheila to try to make others see what she already recognizes – that there is now no sense in avoiding the truth.

Slowly and unwillingly Mrs Birling is forced to admit her part in the tragedy. We should note that the Inspector refers *by name* to Eva Smith, adding 'But Mrs Birling spoke to and saw her only two weeks ago.' After a pause, Mrs Birling says, 'Yes, quite true' (p. 196). She agrees with the Inspector that the girl did not use the name Eva Smith, nor Daisy Renton; she called herself 'Mrs Birling'. What no one notices at that moment is that there is no proof that the so-called 'Mrs Birling' actually was Eva Smith, since only Sheila's mother was shown the photo. This point becomes important in Act Three when Gerald suggests that they may each have been dealing with a different girl.

Mrs Birling proves to be the most reluctant of the family to admit any responsibility, continually defending herself, complaining of the girl's manner, her untrue story and, above all, her impertinence in using the name 'Mrs Birling'. (Obviously she had chosen to use this name because of her relationship with Eric; she could not know that the chairman of the Women's Charity Organization would be Eric's mother!) Mrs Birling insists that she behaved correctly all along; she did her duty and no one will convince her otherwise '. . . because I've done nothing wrong –' (p. 198). Her stubborn attitude provokes the severest response from the Inspector: 'I think you did something terribly wrong – and that you are going to spend the rest of your life regretting it.'

The news that the girl was expecting a baby is a further bombshell for this beleaguered family, and Mrs Birling, in her continuous attempts to shift the blame, moves the story towards its final chapter by her demand that the father of the child be found. The Inspector does not spare her. Since she refuses to admit her own guilt (as Sheila and Gerald have done), he denounces her heartlessness in refusing to help the girl (p. 198). The two reactions to this speech are characteristic: Sheila cries out, 'Mother, I think it was cruel and vile'; but Mr Birling can only think of the damage all this might do to his reputation if it came out at the inquest and the press took it up.

Mrs Birling continues to be strong in her own defence. She enlarges on the responsibility of the unknown father and scorns the girl's story of why she would not marry the young man in question. This attitude rouses the Inspector to his fiercest rebuke: 'Her position now is that she lies with a burnt-out inside on a slab'; and, turning to Birling, who tries to protest, 'Don't stammer and yammer at me again, man. I'm losing all patience with you people . . .' (p. 199).

When people such as Sheila will admit their guilt and express heartfelt regret at what they have done, the Inspector will be calm and even helpful (as when he refuses to allow Sheila to bear all the blame herself). But in the face of people like Mrs Birling who are completely self-righteous and unyielding, he is unsparing in his interrogation and in denouncing their attitude.

The Inspector's outburst persuades Mrs Birling to reveal the details of the girl's story about the father being a silly youngster who drank too much, how she would not marry him since it would be wrong for them both, and how she had refused his money when she learnt it was being stolen. Mrs Birling regains her confidence as she goes over the details and again asserts her old claim that she was quite justified in what she did, holding to the view that the girl had initially shown herself to be a liar and therefore could not be believed at all. Although sorry about the girl's dreadful death, she stoutly declares, 'But I accept no blame for it at all' (p. 200).

This stubborn refusal to see anything wrong in her own actions is going to be heavily punished – and very soon. The Inspector leads her on to place the blame chiefly on the young man who fathered the child: 'He should be made an example of' (p. 200). Soon after, she adds, 'And he ought to be dealt with very severely –'. Sheila is the first to see who this young man must be, and attempts to silence her mother; but Mrs Birling is now very happy that she has (in her view) identified the true culprit and, with a complete lack of charity, she insists that the Inspector does his duty in finding the young man and forcing from him a public confession. It is only when the Inspector agrees and says that for this reason he will wait in their room that the truth dawns on the horrified Mrs Birling and her husband. They — and the audience — wait in suspense for the door to open and thus to have confirmation of what they surely know already. It is Eric who enters the room as the curtain falls on Act Two.

ACT THREE

As on other occasions when a character is about to confess the truth, a squabble springs up between those present. Eric calls Sheila a little sneak for revealing his drinking habits, and both parents attack her for her attitude and her lack of loyalty. These quarrels reflect the anguish of people who are forced to change their whole way of thinking about each other. The Inspector has no time to allow them to indulge in this: 'There'll be plenty of time, when I've gone, for you all to adjust your family relationships,' he says (p. 202).

Under questioning, Eric tells how he met the girl when he was drunk, took her to her lodgings, made love to her, continued the relationship with her and eventually learnt that she was to have his child. Then he tried to help her financially with money stolen from his father's firm. Again various tensions are indicated, as when Eric complains that he is old enough to be married but isn't, and we notice his allusion to his dislike of 'fat old tarts' who go around with some of his father's 'respectable friends' (we recall the behaviour of Alderman Meggarty in the Palace bar). Eric is also offended that the girl treated him like 'a kid' (p. 204). She obviously realized his immaturity and would not trap him into a loveless marriage with someone outside his social class.

Mrs Birling and Sheila return to the room in time to hear Eric explain how he went about stealing his father's money. It leads up to his father's question: 'You damned fool — why didn't you come to me when you found yourself in this mess?' (p. 205). This provokes the shattering reply, 'Because you're not the kind of father a chap could go to when he's in trouble — that's why.' With this remark the guilt of the Birling parents is moved beyond the way they treated Eva Smith. What is now uncovered is their inadequacy as parents. The arrogance of Sheila and the weakness of Eric can be seen as the result of their parents' attitudes and the way they brought up their children.

One more revelation remains: Eric does not know that it was his own mother who finally drove the girl to suicide by refusing her help. The Inspector tells him this with calm authority, and Eric's control breaks completely as he denounces his mother: '. . . you killed her – and the child she'd have had too – my child – your own grandchild – you killed them both – damn you, damn you –' (p. 206). He seems on the point of striking his mother; the family shame and disintegration are complete. Mrs Birling's feeble 'I didn't know – I didn't under-stand' is the classic excuse of those who do great wrong through blindly ignoring the facts in front of them.

From this point, the Inspector takes charge. He is about to leave the house with his work done. He has made the characters face the truth about themselves and reveal it openly, but he has not shown them how to sort out their relationships. As he has already said, there will be plenty of time for that. In his final address to the Birling family (pp. 206–7) he unsparingly reminds each of what he or she did to create the tragedy of Eva Smith. Birling runs true to form when he implies that he would give thousands of pounds if only things could be different, but the Inspector brushes this aside. Each one of them will never forget what he or she has done. But nothing can now help Eva Smith. They cannot even say to her, 'I'm sorry.'

Then the Inspector makes his final remarks and points the moral: '. . . there are millions and millions and millions of Eva Smiths and John Smiths still left with us' and we are responsible for them. 'We don't live alone. We are members of one body. We are responsible for each other' (p. 207). The Inspector departs into the night from whence he came, with the warning that if his lesson is not learnt, then men will be taught it 'in fire and blood and anguish'.

The first words spoken after the Inspector has left come from Birling, and they show clearly that he has learnt nothing. What he does is place the blame firmly on someone else – in this case, Eric – and he shows that what is uppermost in his mind is not the girl's tragedy nor his family's guilt, but his own knighthood: 'Most of this is bound to come out. There'll be a public scandal.' Eric's bitter laughter at this attitude only inflames his anger and Mrs Birling, rapidly reverting to her old self, joins her husband in attacking her son. Sheila is overwhelmed by her parents' reaction: 'The point is, you don't seem to have learnt anything,' she says (p. 208).

For those who think the play may be about to end with the departure of the Inspector, J. B. Priestley has a surprise or two in store. When Eric reminds his father of the way he told the young men after dinner to ignore the cranks 'who tell us everybody has to look after everybody else . . .', he adds that then the Inspector walked in. Sheila, who has already been particularly sensitive to the strangeness of the Inspector, takes up this point at once – 'It's queer – very queer' – and then she utters the key question which has also stirred in Mrs Birling's mind: '. . . but *was* he really a police inspector?' (p. 209). This question dominates the rest of the play.

Once Sheila has put her question, the family becomes sharply divided. For Mr and Mrs Birling, if the Inspector was not a policeman, it could mean that they will avoid a damaging scandal. For Sheila and Eric, on the other hand, the important thing is that the truth has come out and they have acknowledged their responsibility. As Eric says, 'He was our police inspector all right.' Ironically it is Sheila's sensitive awareness of the Inspector which has played into her parents' hands, giving them hope that they have not been visited by the police after all. Birling eagerly latches on to this: the fellow was probably a Socialist or some sort of crank, and they have allowed him to bluff them into confessions. He wants a moment to think out the best course of action, but before he can do so, Gerald returns.

Almost immediately on his return, Gerald is able to answer the outstanding question – was he really a police officer? The answer is no; Gerald has checked with a sergeant of his acquaintance and Mr Birling obtains confirmation of this by phoning the Chief Constable. These men have their answer and are satisfied with it. For Mr Birling the Inspector was a fake, and Gerald agrees: 'We've been had' (p. 212). These expressions are down-to-earth, harsh and insensitive. They entertain no suggestion of the mystery or other-worldliness which Sheila has sensed. Mr Birling and Gerald set about solving the rest of the mystery. Perhaps it was a hoax and they must decide the best way to deal with it.

Against the practical no-nonsense approach, Eric opposes the view that, whoever the Inspector was, each person did what they did to the girl: 'It's what happened to the girl and what we all did to her that matters' (p. 214). Sheila supports him, and despairs that her parents are 'just beginning to pretend all over again'.

The aftermath of the Inspector's visit shows clearly that the older generation – and Gerald – have learnt little. They are certainly more interested in their worldly reputation and the avoidance of scandal than in regretting their treatment of Eva Smith. Only Sheila and Eric seem genuinely affected by the events of the evening, and a huge generation gap opens up between the Birling parents and their children. The older people wish to blot out the whole experience, but the younger ones feel that their lives will never be the same again. Sadly, Gerald takes the side of the older Birlings rather than that of Sheila and Eric. What is more, the clear-thinking Gerald has seen another flaw in what everyone else has been taking for granted.

Continuing the twists and turns of his ingenious plot, J. B. Priestley makes Gerald the mouthpiece for another surprise. Eric has said, 'And it doesn't alter the fact that we all helped to kill her' (p. 215). To this Gerald replies, 'But is it a fact?' He asks what real evidence there is for this. Admittedly they have all been mixed up in a girl's life, '*But how do you know it's the same girl?*' he asks (p. 216). This astonishing thought depends very much on the fact that the Inspector would never allow more than one person at a time to look at the photograph he was showing. As we noted earlier, J. B. Priestley carefully prepared for this moment in Acts One and Two, not only by the handling of the photograph but by never allowing Eva Smith to be too specific in any details she gave about herself. Gerald, of course, saw no picture of a girl, but gave himself away when the name of Daisy Renton was mentioned. But what evidence is there that she was also Eva Smith, except the word of the Inspector, who was not, they now know, a real police inspector? Mrs Birling too accepted that the client who came to her committee was Eva Smith, simply because the Inspector used that name. She said herself that the girl had been simply 'Mrs Birling' to the committee. Only Eric refuses to be convinced: the girl who was expecting a baby whose young father was stealing to support her and who went to a charity committee for help must surely have been the girl he had known. Certainly it would have been a remarkable coincidence for two girls to have been in precisely this situation at the same time and in the same town. But Mr Birling has had another thought – perhaps everything was a put-up job, like the visit of the Inspector himself: 'The whole damned thing can have been a piece of bluff' (p. 217).

Fortunately J. B. Priestley does not have to develop this idea in detail. (It would have needed a very ingenious explanation.) Gerald's assertion that 'There were probably four or five different girls' leads Eric to reply, 'That doesn't matter to me. The one I knew is dead' (p. 218). It is at this point that Mr Birling shows an unexpected quickness of mind and produces the next surprise by asking dramatically, 'Is she? *How do we know she is?*'

The suggestion that perhaps nobody at all has committed suicide is an astonishing development. Mr Birling is elated. If it is true, there will be no inquiry and no scandal and he will be certain to receive his knighthood after all. To settle the matter, Gerald rings the infirmary: the others (and the audience) hold their breath. Then comes the news that they are safe – the infirmary has had no case of suicide for months.

The relief for all the family is enormous, but the lesson of this terrible evening has not been lost on Sheila and Eric. Gerald and the parents are very content to treat the whole thing as an uncomfortable hoax and forget it as soon as possible. But, as Sheila points out, 'Everything we said had happened really had happened' (p. 219). Her father's response is truly shocking. He actually mimics the voice of the Inspector, *'You all helped to kill her'*, and he laughs as he remembers the look on their faces. He goes on to suggest that she reinstates her engagement to Gerald. Sheila, supported by Eric, exclaims passionately against this attempt to ignore the implications of all that has happened and to go on behaving as they did. ('Well, why shouldn't we?' asks the incorrigible Mrs Birling.) The divide between parents and children on this matter is complete, and when Gerald offers Sheila her ring back, it is surprising that she can give him such a controlled answer as she does: 'No, not yet. It's too soon. I must think.' Like her parents, Gerald simply does not understand her – nor the lessons to be learnt from what has happened.

By re-establishing things much as they were, with Mr and Mrs Birling and Gerald quite convinced that nothing has changed nor needs to be changed, J. B. Priestley has prepared the ground for the stunning last lines that bring down the curtain on this remarkable play. The phone rings and Mr Birling answers it.

BIRLING That was the police. A girl has just died – on her way to the infirmary – after swallowing some disinfectant. And a police inspector is on his way here – to ask some – questions.

Characters

MR ARTHUR BIRLING

Mr Birling is a prosperous factory owner, a character modelled on the Bradford industrialists whom J. B. Priestley knew well in his youth. Such men often came from the working class themselves, made money and became rich employers without losing all traces of their origin. Arthur Birling, we are told in the opening stage direction, is 'rather provincial' in his speech and is not the social equal of his wife. We have a clear impression of a self-made man, proud of his achievements in business and civic affairs, confident in himself and in his attitude to others. All this is reflected in his 'fairly easy manners' and his self-important style.

He is a typical example of an employer of the period. His first responsibility is to making a profit. He makes no bones about this: '. . . it's my duty to keep labour costs down' (p. 173). When he welcomes Gerald as his future son-in-law, he sees this family relationship as a prelude to a business link between his firm and that of Gerald's father when 'Crofts and Birlings are no longer competing but are working together – for lower costs and higher prices'. His attitude to a strike among his operatives for a small rise in wages is plain and direct: 'I refused, of course' (p. 172). That the Inspector or anyone else should ask why surprises him. His job is to make money and look after himself.

He makes this the theme of his sermon to Eric and Gerald: '. . . a man has to make his own way – has to look after himself . . . a man has to mind his own business and look after himself and his own –' (p. 168). If he does this he will not come to much harm. What Birling does not consider at all is the harm that may come to other people because of this attitude. He is not unaware that many people would disagree with his philosophy. He knows that the idea that we are all members of a community and should look after each other is gaining increased acceptance. Public speakers and writers like H. G. Wells and Bernard Shaw are spreading such notions, but Birling dismisses these people as 'cranks'. He himself is a 'hard-headed business man' and has 'learnt in the good hard school of experience' (p. 168).

So far nothing has occurred to shake Mr Birling in his beliefs. His business has been successful, he has a comfortable home and what appears on the surface to be a happy family. He has also gained a position in the local community, being a magistrate and a former Lord Mayor. Nor does he see this as the end of the road for himself. When the play opens, he is looking forward to receiving a knighthood, which would set the seal on his career and would provide him with that social status about which he feels insecure. He admits to Gerald that his mother may feel her son is marrying somewhat beneath him socially, but he hopes the knighthood will put that right (p. 167).

What is more, he is enthusiastically optimistic about the future. Speaking in 1912, with the shadow of the First World War approaching, he dismisses all the warnings as simple scare-mongering. The employers are coming together to see that the interests of Capital are properly protected; labour troubles will not amount to anything and, as for the war, there is 'Everything to lose and nothing to gain . . .' (p. 165). It never occurs to him that other motives besides profit and loss could move men to fight.

Mr Birling also has great confidence in the longer term. He believes the new inventions, especially in transport, will usher in a new age of prosperity. Everywhere progress will be rapid, and in twenty or thirty years labour problems and silly little war scares will be all forgotten. What he envisages is the triumph of Capitalism. Significantly he sees only one country lagging behind – Russia, where Communism is soon to triumph (and where *An Inspector Calls* received its first performance).

The events of the play will do much to puncture the self-inflated pomposity and over-confidence of Mr Birling. He is the first to be subjected to the Inspector's questions and he begins by refusing to accept any responsibility: 'If we were all responsible for everything that happened to everybody . . . it would be very awkward, wouldn't it?' (p. 172). He is startled by the Inspector's blunt question, 'Why?' when he speaks of his refusal to raise the wages of his female workers. He is not used to this kind of question, and he is equally irritated when his son seems to be putting the opposing arguments. He certainly does not like the Inspector's attitude, and covertly tries to threaten him by talking of his own friendship with the Chief Constable. His attempts to impress have, of course, no effect on the Inspector.

For Mr Birling the most disturbing disclosures relate to his son, Eric. In the course of the play he discovers that the young man is a drunkard, a thief and has got a girl with child. His own relationship with his son seems in large measure to blame. When he angrily says to Eric, 'You damned fool – why didn't you come to me when you found yourself in this mess?' (p. 205), his son gives the shattering reply, 'Because you're not the kind of father a chap could go to when he's in trouble – that's why.' Birling's response to this accusation is bluster: 'Don't talk to me like that. Your trouble is – you've been spoilt . . .' In other words, he refuses to consider his son's heart–cry and gives not the slightest hint that he is prepared to try to improve their relationship. He is more concerned with getting a list of the accounts Eric has tampered with so that he can cover things up.

Altogether Arthur Birling is an unattractive character. When the Inspector pronounces his final denunciation of the family (p. 207), even Mr Birling is moved to the extent of wishing things were different but his mind goes straight to money: 'Look, Inspector – I'd give thousands – yes, thousands –'. But the Inspector does not allow him to complete his useless thought: 'You're offering the money at the wrong time, Mr Birling' (p. 207).

The odiousness of Birling comes out most clearly in the final moments of the play, when it appears that the Inspector was a hoaxer and that no girl has committed suicide. Ignoring the shameful things his family have undeniably been guilty of, all Mr Birling can think about is the lucky escape from scandal. When Sheila tries to remind him that everything they said has really happened, he insists that 'the whole thing's different now' (p. 219). He is at his worst when he mimics the Inspector ('*You all helped to kill her*') and laughs as he remembers the look on the faces of Eric and Sheila. His old confidence has returned and he mocks 'the famous younger generation who know it all' (p. 220). It is a case of pride coming before a fall; a moment later he is panic-stricken by the news that a girl really has died and an inspector is on his way to question them.

J. B. Priestley has created his character to show the heartlessness of Capitalism, and he allows it no saving grace. A strange visitant, like the Inspector, may reveal the family guilt, but Birling and his wife will not alter their ways, provided their public reputation is safe. The author seems to be implying that the older generation cannot be cured, but that there is a hope that their children may learn the lessons and act differently – though Gerald Croft remains as an example of a younger person very ready to grow into a second Birling.

MRS BIRLING

Mrs Birling is an even less likeable person than her husband. J. B. Priestley describes her in the stage direction (p. 161) as 'a rather cold woman and her husband's social superior'. Both these attributes are borne out in the play. Her awareness of social niceties comes out during the opening conversation, when she gently rebukes her husband for praising the dinner and congratulating the cook. Such things are 'not done'. Later she will approach the Inspector with an assumed graciousness, befitting a lady of good social class. During the dinner party she keeps a quiet control over everything that is happening, smoothing over Sheila's reference to Gerald's absence the previous summer with the comment that men with important work to do sometimes have to devote nearly all their time to it. When the tipsy Eric and his sister seem to be beginning an argument (p. 163), she quickly stops them, urging her husband to propose the toast, and when Eric omits to congratulate the engaged couple, Mrs Birling calls him to order. After her husband's long speech, she attempts to limit his further flow of words, as he acknowledges: 'Yes, my dear, I know – I'm talking too much' (p. 166). These are small details but they establish Mrs Birling as the mistress of the house and someone to be reckoned with.

She withdraws from the dining-room and we see no more of her in Act One. She is not present when the Inspector calls and the involvement of her husband with Eva Smith is revealed, though Mr Birling leaves the room to brief her when Sheila seems to be becoming involved also. She returns to the stage in Act Two when the interrogation of Gerald is just beginning. As J. B. Priestley indicates in the stage direction (p. 185), she is quite out of key with what has just happened. On entering, she gives the impression that she has come to take charge – and also to put a stop to things as soon as possible: '. . . while we'll be glad to tell you anything you want to know, I don't think we can help you much' (p. 185). She maintains this pose despite Sheila's appeals to her to change her attitude. Her snobbishness comes out when she refers to 'girls of that class' (p. 186). To her a working-class girl is an inferior being whom she could not be expected to understand. She also tries to cow the Inspector by criticizing his 'offensive manner' and adding that her husband has been Lord Mayor and is still a magistrate. Altogether she is presenting herself as a confident, upper-class lady, unable to understand why she and her family are being questioned about the affairs of a lower-class suicide.

This confidence takes its first knock when Sheila tells her frankly about Eric's drinking problem, and some strain is evident when she angrily asks the Inspector, 'Well, come along – what is it you want to know?' (p. 188). The revelations by Gerald stagger her, and her first reaction is that such things are not fit for Sheila's ears – an indication that she still regards her daughter as a child. As Gerald's story unfolds she has little to say, listening mostly in silence to what he has done. When Sheila breaks off the engagement, she offers no comment except to conclude that they all have 'just about come to an end of this wretched business' (p. 194). Little does she realize that her own ordeal is just about to begin!

Mrs Birling obviously recognizes the photograph which the Inspector shows her and she realizes the implications, for her first reaction is to try and lie her way out of trouble. But her denial of having seen the girl before cuts no ice with the Inspector. He proceeds with his questions and she, reluctantly and indirectly, admits that she took the chair at the meeting of the Charity Organization a fortnight earlier. Grudgingly she also admits to having seen the girl who called herself 'Mrs Birling'. From now on during the interrogation she fights every step of the way, refusing to accept any blame for influencing the committee to reject the girl's call for help. Her coldness of manner is repellent: the girl had been impertinent to use the name 'Birling'; the girl had told a pack of lies; the girl gave herself 'ridiculous airs'. Nowhere does Mrs Birling show any evidence of sympathy or understanding for the girl's predicament. She insists that she did her duty: '. . . I've done nothing wrong – and you know it' (p. 198). When the Inspector reveals that the girl was pregnant, she is stonily silent until the Inspector asks if she has anything further to tell him. Once again she rejects any suggestion that she might be to blame, preferring to shift the responsibility to the unknown father of the child.

Mrs Birling is undoubtedly shaken by the Inspector's denunciation of her behaviour, surely the most severe rebuke he delivers to any of the characters (p. 198), but she fights back, trying to justify herself as she reveals more and more of what she was told about the girl's reason for refusing marriage and financial help from the child's father. She does have the decency to say she is sorry the girl came to such a horrible end – 'But I accept no blame for it at all' (p. 200). Her unpleasantness is very evident in her vindictiveness towards the young father: '. . . he ought to be dealt with very severely . . . Make sure he's compelled to confess in public his responsibility . . .' (p. 201). This is quite typical of her – a self-righteous denunciation of someone else and a total refusal to see anything wrong in her own conduct. There is swift retribution when she realizes too late that she has denounced her own son!

The first part of Act Three is a time of anguish for Mrs Birling. In the face of Eric's story of his relations with Eva Smith, her confidence crumbles and she is led in tears from the room, but she insists on returning soon after and is told of Eric's stealing from his father's firm. The climax comes when Eric learns that it was his own mother who refused to help the girl and he cries out '. . . your own grandchild – you killed them both – damn you, damn you –' (p. 206) and appears to threaten her physically. Any illusion she may have had of being the mother of a happy family is finally destroyed.

Yet when the Inspector leaves, Mrs Birling 'comes back to life' (in J. B. Priestley's phrase on p. 208) and joins her husband in rebuking Eric. She does show one piece of sensitivity when she agrees with Sheila in feeling there was something strange about the Inspector, but she is quick to support her husband in the view that it would make a great deal of difference if it were shown that the Inspector was not a genuine police officer. As this possibility develops, she gains her old confidence: 'I wish I'd been here when that man first arrived. I'd have asked *him* a few questions . . .' (p. 213). She boasts that she was the only one who did not give in to him. She explains away her own revelations by saying that, being worried by the Inspector's sudden questions, she had answered more or less as he wanted. At the end of the Act she believes that they can all go on behaving just as they did before. She has no time for the attitude of Sheila and Eric, who feel that everything must be different from now on: 'They're over-tired. In the morning they'll be as amused as we are' (p. 220). It is the word 'amused' that is so offensive. How anyone could regard the events of that evening and the tragedy of Eva Smith as 'amusing' passes our comprehension. But Mrs Birling is a cold, hard-hearted and selfish woman. Nothing for long can shake her from her self-righteousness – except possibly the police inspector who is on his way to ask some questions, though knowing Mrs Birling as we do, we can be sure she will give far less away this time round!

SHEILA BIRLING

The author's introductory stage direction describes Sheila as being 'very pleased with life'. She has every reason to be so. She is young and pretty, she is the daughter of a well-to-do family and she has just become engaged to an attractive young man, slightly above her in social class and himself the son of a wealthy manufacturer. Her family have gathered for a celebration dinner, and her fiancé is about to present her with the ring.

Of course there are one or two shadows on her happiness: she does not know why Gerald neglected her for several weeks the previous summer, and she is aware that her brother, Eric, is drinking too much. But these things are not going to interfere with her happiness on this special evening – or so she thinks.

As the play develops, this girl, apparently blessed with every happiness, sees her engagement destroyed, her faith in her family damaged and her own responsibility in a horrible tragedy revealed – above all, to herself. Her reaction to all this is the most heartening thing in the play. We feel that she will genuinely be changed by the experience of the Inspector's visit and that her attitude will encourage her brother to live differently in future, since he also shares her view that there is no going back to the old ways.

Each member of the family contributed to Eva Smith's fate because of a weakness in character. In Sheila's case this was bad temper and jealousy. Eric hints at this as he joins in the good wishes when the toast is drunk to the happiness of Gerald and Sheila: 'All the best! She's got a nasty temper sometimes – but she's not bad really' (p. 164). In such a way does J. B. Priestley prepare the ground for the story of her outburst in Milwards dress shop when it seemed to her that Eva Smith was laughing at her.

Sheila is not present when the Inspector arrives and she does not hear the interrogation of her father. But she is distressed when she learns of the girl's suicide and quickly takes the independent line that is going to separate her from her father and mother. Hearing that her father sacked the girl, she declares firmly, 'I think it was a mean thing to do. Perhaps that spoilt everything for her.' Shortly afterwards, when the Inspector refers to young female workers as 'cheap labour', she cries, 'But these girls aren't cheap labour – they're *people*' (p. 177).

It is with this remark that Sheila places herself firmly on the Inspector's side, even though she does not realize it at the time. Nor is she aware of the dramatic irony that she herself pushed Eva Smith one step further on her path to destruction by demanding her dismissal from Milwards. She learns this very quickly, however, and with a sob rushes from the room. When she returns her first remark is significant: 'You knew it was me all the time, didn't you?' Here is the first hint that Sheila recognizes there is something special about the Inspector. Whoever he is and wherever he obtained his knowledge, he has not come to obtain information. Sheila's cry to Gerald at the end of the act sums it up: 'Why – you fool – *he knows*. Of course he knows. And I hate to think how much he knows that we don't know yet . . .' (p. 182).

There are two important strands in Sheila's character. One is her readiness to acknowledge what she has done wrong. The Inspector has to intervene to prevent her from taking all the blame on herself. The Inspector declares that she is only partly to blame (p. 180), and later on insists that she stays to hear Gerald's part in the affair so that she does not feel she bears the entire guilt, which will leave her 'alone with her responsibility, the rest of tonight, all tomorrow, all the next night –' (p. 184). Associated with this readiness to acknowledge her own fault is an eager desire to do better in future: 'It's the only time I've ever done anything like that, and I'll never, never do it again to anybody' (p. 181).

Sheila, more than any of the other characters, is aware of the mystery of the Inspector. She is the first to realize that 'he knows' everybody's part in the story even before he asks any questions. But when the Inspector makes a moral comment – 'If there's nothing else, we'll have to share our guilt' (p. 184) – she agrees with him but adds (as she looks at him wonderingly), 'I don't understand about you.' What she means is that an ordinary inspector is unlikely to make such a comment. This man has something very special about him and she cannot fathom it. She knows too that in the presence of the Inspector all of them have to 'stop these silly pretences' (p. 187). It is her mother's attempt to behave as she does that horrifies her. The time for polite evasion is over. The truth must come out and guilt must be acknowledged. She recognizes too that the technique of the Inspector is to give them rope so that they themselves confess their part in the tragedy. As she remarks to Gerald, 'Somehow he makes you' (p. 191).

There is a growing desire on Sheila's part to do away with the evasions and half-truths of the past. It is she who tells Mrs Birling of Eric's drinking habits (p. 187), and who speaks bluntly about Alderman Meggarty's reputation with women. When her father protests about the way the Inspector has made Sheila listen to Gerald's confession, Sheila responds with: 'I'm not a child, don't forget. I've a right to know.'

She is also mature in the way she handles the breaking of her engagement. She explains her feelings to Gerald calmly and rationally, and concludes that 'You and I aren't the same people who sat down to dinner here' (p. 194). When at the end of the play Gerald insensitively declares, 'Everything's all right now, Sheila, what about this ring?' she rebuts him with a quiet, 'No, not yet. It's too soon. I must think' (p. 220).

The divide between Sheila (supported by Eric) and her parents comes out most clearly after the Inspector has departed. Her father is entirely occupied in devising ways to avoid a scandal and nothing else matters to him. This shocks Sheila: 'The point is, you don't seem to have learnt anything' (p. 208). Her instinctive feeling that the Inspector may not have been a real police officer does not, for her, alter the important truths that were revealed: 'But don't you see . . . it doesn't much matter who it was who made us confess' (p. 209).

It is she who first casts doubts on the Inspector's identity, but for her this does not make his visit less important. On the contrary, he has done something so tremendous that her life will be changed completely. Only Eric shares this view. The others are excited by the idea that the Inspector's visit was a hoax, and all they want to do is to get back to the old ways as soon as possible. The last pages of the play mirror Sheila's growing desperation at this attitude: 'It frightens me the way you talk . . . You began to learn something. And now you've stopped. You're ready to go on in the same old way' (pp. 219–20). She dramatically recalls the Inspector's words, promising: 'Fire and blood and anguish. And it frightens me the way you talk, and I can't listen to any more of it' (p. 220).

Sheila and her brother represent the younger generation who, J. B. Priestley hopes, may be moved to recognize their responsibility for other people less fortunate than themselves. Sheila's sensitivity to the strangeness of the Inspector, her readiness to accept her share of guilt and her resolve to learn from the experience and act differently in future are the positive qualities which are set against the depressing eagerness of the older generation to forget their sins and go on in the same bad old ways which have already caused disaster.

ERIC BIRLING

Although we are told that Eric, like his sister, is in his early twenties, we have the impression of a very young and immature personality. Unlike his father, who is very much the self-made man, Eric has been given the advantages of an expensive education. The result has not altogether pleased his father, as we see in Act One when Eric dares to ask what was wrong in Eva Smith trying to attain higher wages: 'It's about time you learnt to face a few responsibilities. That's something this public-school-and-Varsity life you've had doesn't seem to teach you' (p. 174). Mr Birling has to learn that the irresponsibility of his son has gone much further than this.

Eric is not entirely at ease during the dinner party. He has had a little too much to drink and suddenly guffaws when, half playfully, Sheila warns Gerald to be careful about neglecting her for the sake of his work. There is no suggestion that Eric has any knowledge of Gerald's affair with Daisy Renton, but his guffaw seems to make an ironic comment on Gerald's promise to take care. Eric can give no explanation for his laugh except that he felt he just had to do it. With hindsight we may feel that Eric is aware that he himself is also concealing a very great deal that he does not want his family to know. At this stage of the play he appears only as an immature younger brother who cannot hold his drink. But his suppressed comment a little later that he remembers something about the importance of clothes to a woman (p. 168) suggests that he is hiding something, and his unease at the news that an Inspector has called at the house reinforces this.

When the interrogation of Mr Birling gets under way and the story of how he sacked Eva Smith is told, Eric irritates his father by saying he thought the girl had been harshly treated and that he (Eric) would not have sacked her. These feelings of sympathy for the girl foreshadow the support he will give to Sheila later in the play when she begs her parents and Gerald to realize that there can be no going back to the old ways.

Eric's responsibility for Eva Smith's tragedy is very great. One night at the Palace bar he had forced his company on the girl, and later he took her home and threatened to make a row if she did not let him come into her room. He admits he was in a 'state when a chap easily turns nasty' (p. 203). It was then that he slept with her for the first time – 'And I didn't even remember – that's the hellish thing. Oh – my God! – how stupid it all is!' He met her two or three times more and then learnt she was to have his baby. In his own way he tried to help her, but she refused to consider marriage since she knew he did not love her. He gave her money, but he had to steal it from his father's firm. From being a drunken young waster he became a seducer and a thief. As the Inspector said in his summing-up, Eric 'Just used her for the end of a stupid drunken evening, as if she was an animal, a thing, not a person' (p. 207). It is a severe indictment.

There can be no excuse for Eric's behaviour, but some understanding of it can be found in his immaturity. Eva Smith recognized this: '. . . she treated me – as if I were a kid' (p. 204). The lack of confidence in his parents is also a factor. When his father asked why he did not come to him for help, he told him frankly that he was not the kind of father a young man in trouble could go to. In his hysterical outburst against his mother when he accuses her of killing her own grandchild, his cry is: 'You don't understand anything. You never did. You never even tried . . .' (p. 206).

After the Inspector has left, Eric accepts his guilt. When his mother self-righteously remarks, 'Eric, I'm absolutely ashamed of you' (p. 208), he takes the rebuke: 'Well, I don't blame you. But don't forget I'm ashamed of you as well – yes, both of you.' From this point onwards he sides with Sheila against his parents and Gerald, who want to avoid scandal and act as if nothing has happened. Although his sister takes the lead, he speaks at length for both of them (p. 214). It makes no difference if the Inspector was real or not: 'It's still the same rotten story . . . The money's not the important thing. It's what happened to the girl and what we all did to her that matters.' Eric has certainly learnt his lesson. A spoilt and weak-charactered offspring of unattractive parents he may be, but at the end of the play we feel that for him, as for Sheila, his view of life and of his responsibility for other people is going to be altogether different in future.

GERALD CROFT

J. B. Priestley describes Gerald Croft as 'an attractive chap about thirty, rather too manly to be a dandy, but very much the easy well-bred young man-about-town'. This neatly characterizes Gerald for us at the beginning of the play, but a great deal more about him and the sort of person he is emerges as the play proceeds.

At first he seems an admirable future husband for Sheila. Not only attractive personally, he is very acceptable as a son-in-law to Sheila's parents. He is the son and heir of a rival manufacturer whose family is somewhat socially superior to the Birlings. His father already has a knighthood and so, from the Birling point of view, he is a good catch, especially since the marriage promises business links between the two firms. What is more, Gerald's attitude to business methods is similar to Mr Birling's. He thoroughly sympathizes with the older man's view that, as a ringleader in the strike, Eva Smith had to be sacked. 'You couldn't have done anything else,' he says (p. 173), adding later that he is sure he and his father would have done the same thing if faced with the problem in their own firm.

His confidence that he himself had nothing to do with the death of Eva Smith is severely shaken when he is told that she changed her name to Daisy Renton, and his instinct is to hush the matter up and pretend ignorance. Sheila is in no doubt that his reaction to the girl's assumed name has completely given him away and that Daisy Renton was the reason for Gerald's neglect of her the previous summer. Gerald's cowardly appeal to her to help him keep this from the Inspector is met with her scornful 'Why – you fool – *he knows.*'

The assurance of Gerald cracks rapidly when the Inspector returns to the room. The young man makes an attempt to persuade Sheila to leave the room so that she will not hear the sordid details of his affair, and he reveals a certain spitefulness when he accuses Sheila of only wanting to stay so that she can see him being 'put through it' by the Inspector, just as she has been. She rightly feels that if he had really loved her, he could never have said that. Already it appears that real love was not involved in his proposed marriage, and we are not surprised that at the end of the play it seems unlikely that it will take place.

Gerald's relationship with Daisy Renton is perhaps the least blameworthy of all of them. Sheila herself admits this when she says, '. . . you came out of it better than the rest of us' (p. 215). He began by rescuing the girl from the unwelcome attentions of Alderman Meggarty, took her to a hotel for a drink and, finding she was so poor that she was lacking food, provided her with a meal. The next time they met he found she was about to be evicted from her room because she could not pay the rent and so he installed her in a set of rooms a friend had lent him for six months. So far his behaviour towards the girl had been praiseworthy: 'I was sorry for her . . . I didn't ask for anything in return' (p. 191).

All the same, when the girl obviously fell in love with him, he did not resist, despite his relationship with Sheila. Daisy Renton became his mistress and the affair continued until he broke it off in the September before he went away on business for several weeks. He provided the girl with money to last her the rest of the year.

Gerald's guilt is crisply summarized by Sheila: 'Gerald set her up as his mistress and then dropped her when it suited him' (p. 195). It also involved him in lying to Sheila and betraying the love he was supposed to have for her. The Inspector acknowledges that Gerald 'at least had some affection for her and made her happy for a time' (p. 207), but by discarding her with only limited money he made almost inevitable her return to the Palace bar where later she met Eric.

We might have been able to view Gerald with at least some sympathy if he had not been so eager towards the end of the play to identify himself with Mr and Mrs Birling and their efforts to cancel out the effects of the Inspector's visit. He is an intelligent young man and, given the opportunity to chat to a police sergeant during his walk, he established that Inspector Goole was unknown to the local police force, a fact quickly verified by Mr Birling's call to the Chief Constable. When Birling declares that this makes all the difference, Gerald enthusiastically agrees, in clear opposition to the attitude of Sheila and Eric. He is also shrewd enough to spot the possibility that there is no certainty that they have all been dealing with the same girl, for the photograph was only shown to one person at a time. He is quick to support Mr Birling when he extends the argument to the point of querying whether *any* girl has died after all. Gerald is the one who rings the infirmary and then is able to announce that no girl has died there that day; he is clearly relieved and satisfied at his discovery. He remains silent while Sheila and Eric are desperately appealing for the others not to reject what the Inspector has taught them. He reveals which side he is on when he blandly says, 'Everything's all right now, Sheila. What about this ring?' (p. 220). With these words he dismisses all that Sheila has been saying. It is an invitation to her to return to the old ways and forget the events of the evening. Under the circumstances her reply is surprisingly controlled: 'No, not yet. It's too soon. I must think' (p. 220). We must wonder if it will ever be possible to bridge the gap between them.

INSPECTOR GOOLE

Whoever he is and wherever he comes from, Inspector Goole presents a very solid appearance when he enters the Birling household. He gives an impression of 'massiveness, solidity and purposefulness' and his speech is careful and weighty. At first there is nothing to suggest that he is not a typical stage detective, calm and authoritative in manner and rather daunting to those with anything to hide. His answers to Mr Birling's attempts to get on terms with him are almost curt and he gives nothing away. When he states his business, it is brief and factual – though he makes sure that the horror of the girl's suicide registers: 'Burnt her inside out, of course . . . she was in great agony' (p. 170).

As he begins his questioning a slightly menacing quality enters his manner, although superficially he is always correct. The first hint of this menace is when he keeps the photograph away from Gerald and Eric and, when asked by Gerald if there is any reason why he should not see the girl's picture, he replies '[*coolly, looking hard at him*]: There might be' (p. 171). His further explanation that he prefers to deal with one person at a time and with one line of inquiry is plausible, but does not remove the unease that his remark has created. This of course is part of the Inspector's technique. By stirring guilty memories with his photograph and questions, he leads each character in turn to acknowledge publicly things they had expected to keep hidden. What is more, he intends to show how one isolated incident can be part of a chain of events with incalculable consequences.

The first time the Inspector moves beyond his role as an ordinary police investigator is when, following Birling's account of how he sacked Eva Smith, he asks the stark question, 'Why?' It is hardly police business to ask an employer the reason why he sacked a worker, and Birling has every cause to be surprised at the question. When a little later he says that some workers would soon be asking for the earth, the Inspector replies, 'They might. But after all it's better to ask for the earth than to take it' (p. 173). Here again he is making a comment on Birling's social attitudes in a way which is quite untypical of a police officer. He speaks in a similar vein to Sheila, remarking '. . . I've thought that it would do us all a bit of good if sometimes we tried to put ourselves in the place of those young women counting their pennies in their dingy little back bedrooms' (p. 177).

The Inspector's method of investigation is well illustrated in his encounter with Sheila. He gives a factual account of the incident at Milwards, thereby stirring the guilty memory of Sheila, shows her a picture of the girl which she recognizes, and leaves her to acknowledge the part she has played. When Birling asks him why he is upsetting his daughter like this, he replies, 'I didn't do it. She's upsetting herself' (p. 178). Sheila, who at first ran out of the room, returns to tell her story. The Inspector quietly feeds her one or two leading questions, but it is Sheila who does most of the talking. Only at the end of it does he frame an accusation: 'And so you used the power you had . . . to punish the girl just because she made you feel like that?' (p. 181).

Towards the end of Act One the Inspector gives an explanation of his visit. Having seen the dead girl, he said to himself: ' "Well, we'll try to understand why it had to happen." And that's why I'm here, and why I'm not going until I know *all* that happened' (p. 181). In this way he will fulfil the role which J. B. Priestley has designed for him – namely, to show how a series of unrelated acts of selfishness can form a chain of events to bring a fellow creature to destruction when we ignore or reject the argument that we are all responsible for one another.

What is unnerving about the Inspector is the fact that, although he asks questions, he seems already to know the full story – at any rate in outline. Sheila is the first to realize this: 'You knew it was me all the time, didn't you?' (p. 179). At the end of Act One she cries out to Gerald, 'Why – you fool – *he knows*' (p. 182). She is also aware that attempts to hide things from the Inspector will only make matters worse. Her mother shocks her by trying to do just that, and Mrs Birling's attempt to shift the blame to the baby's unknown father leads to the terrible discovery that she has been denouncing her own son and has contributed to the death of her unborn grandchild. The Inspector is particularly severe with Mrs Birling because she is the most stubborn in refusing to acknowledge her responsibility. This comes later in the play, but at their first encounter Mrs Birling experiences the effects of the Inspector's technique when she learns from Sheila of Eric's drinking. She exclaims, 'But it's you – and not the Inspector here – who's doing it –' (p. 187). This is very much what we have come to expect: the Inspector places the characters in a situation where all pretences have to be swept away. Those, like Mrs Birling, who resist will suffer most in the end.

As more and more of the truth is revealed, friction inevitably breaks out between the characters. The Inspector will not allow this to affect his investigation. He cuts in on the tetchy exchange between Gerald and Sheila as she begins her story with, 'Never mind about that. You can settle that between you afterwards' (p. 180), and at the beginning of Act Three he says to the quarrelling Birlings, 'There'll be plenty of time, when I've gone, for you all to adjust your family relationships' (p. 202).

The Inspector is also careful to prevent any one character from bearing the full burden of guilt. Sheila is very prone to do this, but the Inspector insists that she is only partly to blame and that is why he wants her to listen to Gerald's story. He pronounces no judgement on what Gerald has to say, as the young man is obviously aware of the effect of his desertion of the girl. But with Mrs Birling he does not mince words – 'I think you did something terribly wrong' (p. 198) – and a few moments later he crushingly denounces her when she tries to pass on responsibility to the child's father in his speech beginning, 'That doesn't make it any the less yours . . .' (p. 198). Yet even this does not subdue Mrs Birling, and she brings the Inspector to the point of losing his temper: 'Her position now is that she lies with a burnt-out inside on a slab. [*As* BIRLING *tries to protest* . . .] Don't stammer and yammer at me again, man. I'm losing all patience with you people . . . (p. 199).

Like his sister, Eric recognizes the Inspector's knowledge of what has happened. 'You know, don't you,' he says at the beginning of Act Three. As with Sheila, all the Inspector has to do is ask plain questions to enable Eric to reveal his own responsibility. The chain of events is almost complete. Only Mrs Birling's inability to confess to Eric what she has done leads the Inspector to state her part for her. Eric's hysterical breakdown marks the final disintegration of the family unity shown in the dinner party with which the play opened. Now the Inspector cuts across the chaos of anger and recrimination with a resounding '*Stop!*' In the tense calm that follows, he allocates the share in the responsibility for Eva Smith's death to each one and ends with the voice of a prophet: 'We don't live alone. We are members of one body. We are responsible for each other. And I tell you that the time will soon come when, if men will not learn that lesson, then they will be taught it in fire and blood and anguish. Good night' (p. 207).

The Inspector walks out of the house, leaving them to recover their balance and then evaluate his visit. The question as to who he really was seems vital to Mr and Mrs Birling and Gerald, but to Sheila and Eric it is immaterial: 'Well, he inspected us all right . . . Between us we drove that girl to commit suicide' (p. 215). The Inspector has called and gone. He appeared to be seeking answers to questions, but his knowledge of everyone's guilt seemed to be complete before he began. His task was to make the characters acknowledge what he already knew, and his motive was to preach a message of social responsibility in the face of selfishness and greed. From being merely an investigator, he moved on to be a commentator, an accuser, a judge and finally a prophet announcing doom to a world that will not hear his message. It is the fate of a prophet to be accepted by some but to be rejected by the majority, and this is what happens at the end of the play. Sheila and Eric will be different: their parents and Gerald will see no reason for change. But a real inspector is about to call. Will this make any difference? We have no confidence that it will. The world is still going to be a harsh place for all the Eva Smiths as long as the Birlings are in control. But we are left with just a hope that in time the Sheilas and Erics of this world may do things differently and that the Inspector will not have called in vain.

EVA SMITH

Eva Smith never appears on the stage, yet every character in the play (apart from the Inspector and the maid) has some responsibility for her tragedy and she is a very real presence in the action from beginning to end. Of course doubts have been raised about the identity of the girl. Was it one and the same girl whom each of the family met, or did each meet a different one, as Gerald suggested (p. 216)? Was Daisy Renton also Eva Smith, and was she the girl who called herself 'Mrs Birling' when she appeared before the Women's Charity Organization? Most dubious of all, did she – or anyone else – commit suicide and die that day in the infirmary? In the last minutes of the play this idea seems quite untrue, but the final phone message from the police speaks of a girl who really has died and whose suicide is prompting police inquiries at the Birling home. Is this dead girl Eva Smith or someone else? The mystery is all part of the play and – like the identity of the Inspector – is never solved. But in the minds of the audience a very clear picture emerges of the girl who is at the centre of everyone's thoughts, and we seem to know as much about her as any other character.

Assuming we are considering one and the same girl, we can build up quite a full portrait of her. She was very pretty, with big dark eyes and soft brown hair – pretty enough certainly for Sheila to be jealous of her and for both Gerald and Eric to be attracted to her. Mr Birling remembers her as 'a lively good-looking girl – country-bred, I fancy'

(p. 172). The Inspector adds a little later that both her parents were dead and she had no home to go back to. She had come to the city to find work and had done so at Birling's factory. Here she gained a reputation as a good worker and the foreman was ready to promote her to be leading operator. Her leadership qualities, however, came out in a different way when she took an important part in organizing a strike for higher pay. Birling recalls that, in his view, she had far too much to say and so he sacked her.

Already a picture is developing of an attractive girl with a strong personality, qualities of leadership and an independent mind. Two months out of work, half-starved and friendless, she was reduced to desperation, but the lucky chance of a job at Milwards promised a fresh start. Once again we are told that she was a satisfactory worker. She was unfortunate to be caught smiling when Sheila tried on the dress, and for that she paid dearly.

Lacking any employment, she had started hanging around the Palace bar – a well-known spot for girls to be picked up by men. It was from the unwelcome attentions of one such man – Alderman Meggarty – that Gerald rescued her. He found her to be warm-hearted and very grateful for the way he had helped her. In fact he admits that she regarded him as her Fairy Prince. For Daisy Renton (as she now called herself) her months with Gerald were the happiest time in her life, and it is obvious that she was in love with him. When the affair ended, she went away to a seaside town, largely to savour the memory of her life with Gerald – in the words of her diary, 'just to make it last longer' (p. 193). As we might expect, she took Gerald's announcement that their relationship must end calmly and was 'very gallant' about it, knowing that it could not last.

The wretchedness of her situation as well as her fine personal qualities are to be seen clearly in her dealings with Eric. She was reluctant to encourage him into a love affair, but at their first meeting, in his drunkenness he forced himself on her. Other meetings followed. The news that she was to have his baby was a crisis in her life. She might well have gone to his parents and insisted on marriage or else a large sum of money to hush the matter up. But she did not: she refused to consider marriage because she knew he did not love her. When she realized that the money Eric was giving her was stolen, she refused this also and told him she did not want to see him again. Eric admits that, although she was not much older

than he was, she was far more mature: 'In a way, she treated me —
as if I were a kid' (p. 204).

J. B. Priestley creates the portrait of a girl of strong character and
high principles who, in her desperate straits, will not further embroil
the weak young man who is responsible for her condition. When she
goes to the Women's Charity Organization for help she has some
pride left, for she pretends at first that she is married and has been
deserted by her husband. But when the truth comes out that she is
refusing money from the father of the child in order to stop him
stealing, she is not believed. There is nothing left for her, she feels,
except suicide.

It is a tragic story of a girl more attractive and with better qualities
than anyone else in the play who is brought to destruction by the
heartlessness and selfishness of others.

Commentary

WHO IS THE INSPECTOR?

This is an irrelevant question – even though we are bound to turn it over in our minds. Frankly, it does not matter in the least who the Inspector is. The important point about him is what he does to the Birling family and, by extension, to the audience. His function is to stir us to examine our consciences (as he did the Birlings) and to make us more sharply aware of our social responsibilities. His visit shows in a highly dramatic way how anything from a quick fit of temper to a shameful episode lasting several months (but now suppressed in our minds) can help to destroy a fellow human being.

J. B. Priestley gives no hint in the play as to who the Inspector is nor where he comes from. He is a figure of fantasy and no rational explanation is possible. The playwright was not a religious man and there is no suggestion that the Inspector is in any way a messenger from God – despite the biblical tone of his warning that those who ignore his message 'will be taught it in fire and blood and anguish' (p. 207) and despite the Christian echo in the same speech: 'We are members of one body.'

Some people may speculate that the Inspector is the voice of each character's individual conscience. Certainly he does stir people's consciences to admit personal guilt, but his effect is limited, since only Sheila and Eric are prepared to change their attitudes in the future, when the identity of the Inspector becomes doubtful.

Despite its realistic style, naturalistic set and characters recognizably from ordinary life, the play is a fantasy. It is quite incredible that no less than five people, all connected with one family, should have each individually damaged one and the same girl – and done so without the others knowing anything about it. Equally incredible is the alternative that as many as five different girls might have been involved. This is not said as a criticism of the play, but to stress the fact that the play is not to be considered as a piece of realism and therefore it is pointless to search for an 'explanation' of the Inspector. What he does within the play is explanation enough.

WHAT WILL HAPPEN WHEN THE REAL INSPECTOR CALLS?

Again this question – although an intriguing one – lies beyond the scope of the play. What has been established is that once the fear of public exposure has been removed, Mr and Mrs Birling and Gerald have no further problem in coping with their guilty memories and are quite ready to return to their old attitudes. Only Sheila and Eric seem prepared to learn a lesson from the Inspector's visit. This is the final point that J. B. Priestley makes in his play – that even when guilt is clearly placed upon them, many people will brush it aside as soon as it poses no danger to the continuance of their old selfish way of life.

The news in the last lines of the play that an undoubted police inspector is on his way to ask the family some questions renews the danger of scandal which Mr Birling thought he had avoided – hence his panic-stricken look when he answers the phone. What will ensue when the real inspector arrives is purely a matter for speculation. (It might be an interesting exercise for students of the play to draft out possible scenarios based on a knowledge of the characters and their attitudes shown in the play itself.) One cannot help feeling that – warned by their previous experience – Mr and Mrs Birling will be very much more cautious before they admit any responsibility whatsoever and will do all they can to prevent Sheila and Eric from blurting out anything embarrassing. It is worth remembering – and Mr Birling in a calm moment would certainly think of this – that none of the characters except Eric (who has stolen money) has done anything *criminal*. Here again we are reminded of the message of the play, namely that it is our social sins – selfishness, inconsiderateness, the using of other people for our own pleasure – that cause so many tragedies in the world. We may remember that Gerald's declaration, 'We're respectable citizens and not criminals,' brings the retort from the Inspector, 'Sometimes there isn't as much difference as you think. Often, if it was left to me, I wouldn't know where to draw the line' (p. 179).

By announcing that a girl has died and that a real police inspector is coming to the house, J. B. Priestley has provided a wonderfully dramatic ending to his play, calling into doubt once more the Birlings' arrogant assumption of safety from scandal. Does it contain a foreshadowing of the swift retribution and of the 'anguish' (if not the 'fire and the blood') which Inspector Goole promised to those who ignored his message?

STRUCTURE

An Inspector Calls gains a great deal of its force from the very compact structure of the play. Nothing is allowed to distract from the central thrust of the action. The play takes place in one location, the action is virtually continuous and there is no sub-plot. In earlier centuries, critics praised an author if he observed what they called the Unities – those of place, time and action. They would have been well satisfied with J. B. Priestley's structure.

Act One introduces us to the characters and establishes the idea of a happy and united family facing the future with confidence and self-satisfaction. Despite some carefully planted hints that all is not as it seems, there is nothing to prepare us for the shock of the Inspector's visit. His business is quickly stated and the involvement of Mr Birling and Sheila in the tragedy of Eva Smith is revealed. The act ends with the promise of further revelations, particularly about Gerald.

Our curiosity about Gerald is not immediately satisfied at the beginning of Act Two. Attention at first focuses largely on Mrs Birling, whose self-confidence is shaken by the revelation of Eric's drinking. Tension rises with Sheila's growing awareness that everyone is becoming implicated: '. . . he is giving us rope – so that we'll hang ourselves' (p. 188). Then we learn Gerald's story of his affair with Daisy Renton, and this is followed at once by the battle with Mrs Birling to extract the truth of her involvement with the girl. Her attempt to shift the blame on to someone else leads her to denounce the father of the girl's unborn child, and the act ends with his entrance: Eric stands in the doorway.

Act Three completes the revelations, with the involvement of Eric fully explained. The Inspector speaks his final judgement and departs. The decks are cleared for the family to react to the new situation and to re-adjust their relationships. In the event, the idea is developed that the Inspector's visit was a hoax and the very existence of Eva Smith is called in question. The moral divide between the parents and Gerald on the one hand and Sheila and Eric on the other is confirmed. The play ends with a phone call announcing that a police inspector is on his way to ask some questions about a girl who has just died in the infirmary.

STAGECRAFT

J. B. Priestley was a master craftsman, and by the time he wrote *An Inspector Calls* he had had some fifteen years' experience as a playwright. His skill is obvious in the tight construction of the play, its swift development and its ability to maintain the element of surprise to the very last lines.

In essence, the play is a thriller, an unusual kind of 'whodunit', with Eva Smith as the dead victim and the gradual unravelling of the mystery of her death by a stage detective – in this case, the Inspector. The success or failure of a thriller depends to some extent on how far we are able to take seriously the involvement of each of the characters. In *An Inspector Calls* we are bound to take them very seriously indeed, because the crime is a social crime and one in which we may all see our own faults reflected.

Success also depends on startling the audience with unexpected developments that nevertheless fit into a convincing pattern until the whole amazing story is told and curiosity finally satisfied, as it will be most effectively if the least likely person is shown to be the guilty party. In this play everyone is guilty, and so J. B. Priestley begins by showing how secure and self-satisfied they feel themselves to be, yet signalling to the audience that all is not quite as it seems. We see that Eric is tipsy, we learn of Sheila's quick temper, and there is a reference to Gerald's neglect of his fiancée during the previous summer.

The most striking indication that the Birlings are far less secure than they imagined comes in Mr Birling's long speech expressing confidence in the future of Capitalism, which will bring increasing prosperity to them all. The possibility of war is contemptuously dismissed. Yet the audience know that only two years later the First World War will break out and the world as Mr Birling knew it will be gone for ever. By allowing him to voice this colossal misjudgement, J. B. Priestley casts doubt on every assumption about his life and family that Mr Birling has been making. In this way the audience is prepared to see this unpleasantly proud man humbled, though how it will be done remains unclear.

The arrival of the Inspector is the first of a long series of surprises. The last thing that anyone would expect at an engagement party is a visit from the police, and the news that a girl's suicide might be connected with this solidly respectable family is intriguing, to say the least. The audience expects revelations and it begins to get them. At first the pace is fairly leisurely: Mr Birling is shown a photograph which he recognizes as that of a girl he once employed and subsequently dismissed. The audience notices that Gerald and Eric are not allowed to see the photo. As early as this, Eric begins to express opposition to his father's view on how to deal with a strike leader. The solid structure of the Birling family is beginning to shake a little. Then Sheila is shown to be involved in the dead girl's story, and the audience becomes aware that more and more of the household are going to be caught up by the investigation. This feeling becomes a certainty when Gerald reacts to the photograph which his father is shown. Everyone seems to have a skeleton in the cupboard and the cupboard doors are opening.

By the end of Act One, the skill with which J. B. Priestley has set the scene, established his characters and begun to piece together the jigsaw of Eva Smith's last year is very evident. At the centre of the action he has placed the strong, rather forbidding and already mysterious figure of the Inspector. Two characters have unexpectedly been forced to acknowledge a connection with Eva Smith. As the first act ends, a third character – Gerald – also admits being involved. The curtain falls.

Knowing how and when to end an act effectively is one mark of a good playwright. J. B. Priestley's use of the curtain in this play is masterly. As the first act is coming to an end, he implicates Gerald in the story of Eva Smith (or Daisy Renton). Unlike Mr Birling and Sheila, Gerald believes he can hide his part from the Inspector. He confesses only to Sheila and begs her to keep his secret. The strangeness of the Inspector is crystallized for the audience in Sheila's cry, 'Why – you fool – *he knows. Of course he knows . . .*' (p. 182). As she looks at him almost in triumph, the door slowly opens (always a moment of mystery!) and there stands the Inspector with the accusing word, 'Well?' The curtain falls, cutting off any answer and leaving the audience agog for the revelation that must follow after the interval. By beginning the second act with that same word, 'Well?', the author gains the best of both worlds: he has the dramatic effect of the fall of the curtain and also the impression of complete continuity of action.

Act Two does not satisfy our curiosity about Gerald immediately: J. B. Priestley knows the effect of keeping us waiting in anticipation. First there is the rift between Gerald and Sheila. The girl's puzzlement over the identity of the Inspector is developed. Then the mood is unexpectedly changed by Mrs Birling's arrival and her attempt to deal with the Inspector in a way which is quite out of tune with the new atmosphere of guilt and doubt. There are shocks in store for her as the news of Eric's drinking and of Gerald's affair with Daisy Renton is revealed. In such ways does the author hold the attention of the audience as he approaches the climax of the act, where he shows that Mrs Birling herself had dealings with the girl. The most unpleasant of all the characters, Mrs Birling might seem the least likely to have known Eva Smith. Yet the net of her own guilt is drawn around her, twist and turn as she may. Then fatally she shifts the blame to the unknown father of Eva Smith's child. Sheila suddenly realizes what the audience must also have guessed by now. Only one character remains uninvolved; only one story remains to be told. We wait for the door to open. When it does so, Eric enters – and the curtain falls. Once again the dramatic effect of the curtain is considerable.

As between the previous acts, there is no time-gap. When the curtain rises on Act Three, the action begins immediately from where it left off with Eric's entrance. Now the final piece of the jigsaw is in place and the whole of Eva Smith's story is known. But the excitement arises less from this than from the breakdown of the Birling family, with Eric's terrible cursing of his mother and then the final pronouncement of the Inspector. He departs into the night and, if this were an ordinary thriller, the play would swiftly come to an end, since the whole story of why Eva Smith died and who was responsible is now explained.

J. B. Priestley, however, now brings us to the real point of the play: how will each of the characters react to the events of the evening? At first there is the expected squabble, but with great cunning he makes Eric bitterly remind his father that just as he was denouncing 'cranks' one of them walked in. This provokes Sheila into wondering if the man really was a police inspector. Suddenly the play takes a new turn: supposing the whole thing was a hoax? Mr and Mrs Birling see hope of avoiding scandal and their spirits rise. Then, with the audience closely following the speculations, Gerald comes on to confirm that the man was certainly *not* from the police. The author now has us all eager to know who the Inspector was and if Mr and Mrs Birling, with Gerald, are going to be able to sweep aside the scruples of Sheila and Eric and return to safety – and their old attitudes. But with his flair for maintaining tension, the author has three more surprises in store.

First he makes Gerald question whether they have all been involved with the same girl. A new and startling thought indeed, but one which J. B. Priestley has carefully prepared by making the Inspector allow only one person at a time to see the photo. Next, the author sets the characters arguing the pros and cons of this suggestion until Mr Birling wakes up to where it is logically leading: if they cannot be sure it was only one girl, how do they know it was *any* girl who died? A quick phone call to the infirmary confirms the idea. There never was a suicide after all and the whole thing was an elaborate hoax. This development has enabled the author to make the moral positions of the various characters absolutely clear: Mr and Mrs Birling, supported by Gerald, want to laugh the whole thing off, while Sheila and Eric insist that guilt has been acknowledged and everything must be different in future. They seem to be on the losing side, sickeningly aware that for their parents and Gerald nothing has changed at all. Mr Birling is riding high as he laughs at 'the famous younger generation who know it all. And they can't even take a joke –'. The author has given the appearance of victory to the proud and the selfish but, with infinite skill, he has really prepared for their fall and the final surprise of this exciting play. The phone rings and the news comes that a police inspector is on his way to ask some questions. Guilty and

dumbfounded, the characters stare at one another as another play –
unwritten – awaits to unfold.

PARENTS AND CHILDREN

The play reveals among the shortcomings of Mr and Mrs Birling
their failure as parents. Outwardly the Birlings are a happy and
united family, with an expensively educated son just finding his feet
in his father's business and an attractive daughter about to become
engaged to a highly suitable young man. Such parents would have
every reason to congratulate themselves on the way they had brought
up their children.

The reality is different: unknown to his parents, Eric is a weak-
willed drunkard who has got a girl into trouble and has taken to
stealing to provide her with money. Sheila has not hesitated to use her
social position to force a working-class girl out of her job because of
some slight to her pride. Both young people have good qualities, as
we know, but their parents have no contact with them at any deep
level. They fail to take them seriously as adults and, in a crisis, can
offer them no support worth having.

Although Sheila is a young woman of marriageable age, her parents
are prone to treat her as a child, feeling she should not be exposed to
the sordidness of real life. Mr Birling says, 'I see no point in mentioning the subject . . .' (in front of Sheila) when Gerald talks of the
women of the town haunting the Palace bar. His wife is very shocked
when Sheila frankly describes the behaviour of old Meggarty towards
a girl she knows. Mrs Birling excuses Eric's drinking with 'He's only
a boy', unaware of the true state of his alcoholism. Birling protests at
the way his daughter '. . . a young unmarried girl, is being dragged
into this –' (p. 192). For this he is rebuked by the Inspector and by
Sheila herself. 'I'm not a child, don't forget,' she tells him.

The divide between the generations is sharpened by Eric's bitter
accusation of his parents for the way their selfish attitudes have
contributed to his own personal disasters. Mr Birling's idea of
bringing up a child was to surround him with material wealth, pay for
an expensive education, and allow him 'more money to spend and
time to spare' than when he was Eric's age (p. 168). But real sympathy

and understanding have been lacking, and when a crisis came the young man had no one to turn to because Mr Birling was 'not the kind of father a chap could go to when he's in trouble' (p. 205). Eric's judgement on his mother is even more severe. After his outburst against her for killing both the girl and her child, he over-rides her feeble 'I didn't know – I didn't understand' with a caustic 'You don't understand anything. You never did. You never even tried . . . (p. 206).

It is hard to see how any real family relationship can be built without complete openness and a readiness to learn honestly about each other. But Mr and Mrs Birling show no sign of wanting to achieve this once it appears to them that the Inspector's visit was a hoax. Mr Birling laughs as he remembers the look on their faces when the Inspector said, 'You all helped to kill her,' and he assures Sheila that she will have 'a good laugh over it yet' (p. 219). Mrs Birling remarks that the children are 'over-tired. In the morning they'll be as amused as we are' (p. 220). These parents show not the slightest comprehension of the effect which the Inspector has had on Eric and Sheila. The intense seriousness of his children provokes Birling to the crude sneer about 'the famous younger generation who . . . can't even take a joke'. Then the phone rings and he learns that a real inspector is on his way. For him, the joke is over.

There is no attempt on the part of J. B. Priestley to excuse Sheila nor to spare Eric for what they contributed to Eva Smith's destruction, but we are shown the inadequacy – to say the least – of the upbringing and education which provided the Birling children with so much material wealth but left them bereft of a sense of responsibility towards those less fortunate than themselves. But Sheila and Eric, unlike their parents, are prepared to admit their guilt and change their ways. This may be a reflection of the hope of so many people in 1946 that the younger generation would build a new world, avoiding the errors that had led to the World War which had just ended with Europe in ruins and Japanese cities devastated by the atom bombs.

A CHAIN OF EVENTS

Considered individually, none of the faults committed by the characters in the play would have been likely to drive a girl to suicide. For a factory boss to sack a strike leader was considered – at any rate by his associates – as a sensible thing to do; a shop girl, dismissed for upsetting a customer, would not be expected to swallow disinfectant, nor would a discarded mistress. No charity organization who doubted the claims of an applicant would feel they were driving her to suicide by refusing her help, nor would the young man who had fathered a child feel he was condemning its mother to death when she declined to marry him and sent him out of her life. Each of these events was certainly serious enough for the recipient, but none could be expected to produce the ghastly end of Eva Smith.

For each of the characters the involvement with Eva Smith was a single event, over and done with, and of no significance in their present lives. Mr Birling voiced this view when he said, 'It's a perfectly straightforward case, and as it happened more than eighteen months ago – nearly two years ago – obviously it has nothing to do with the wretched girl's suicide' (p. 172). But the Inspector disagrees. He is of the opinion that 'what happened to her then may have determined what happened afterwards, and what happened to her afterwards may have driven her to suicide. A chain of events.' Birling acknowledges that there may be something in this, but comments that it would be very awkward 'if we were all responsible for everything that happened to everybody'. The Inspector echoes him: 'Very awkward,' he says. Yet the point J. B. Priestley is making in this play is precisely this. We *should* consider our individual actions and the effect they may have on other people's lives. A minor misdeed, a lack of sympathy, a piece of selfishness may well begin a chain of events which could lead a person to tragedy. The author is pleading for acknowledgement of the proposition that we should feel responsible for other people in the world – 'the millions and millions and millions of Eva Smiths and John Smiths' that the Inspector refers to in his final speech.

It is the absolutely opposite view of Mr Birling, who preaches that a man 'has to look after himself – and his family too, of course . . . and so long as he does that he won't come to much harm'. Birling dismisses as cranks those who talk and write 'as if we were all mixed up together like bees in a hive . . .' (p. 168). Yet this involvement of each of us in the whole of mankind is the very thing to which J. B. Priestley is drawing our attention. If any one of the characters had treated Eva Smith differently, the terrible chain of events would have been broken and her tragedy might have been averted. The fact that there is some doubt over the identity of both Eva Smith and the Inspector is irrelevant to the author's purpose — which is to urge us to look more closely at our own actions and consider the effect they may have on other people, especially those less happily placed than ourselves. 'We are responsible for each other' (p. 207).

AVOIDING THE BLAME

As *An Inspector Calls* unfolds, one has an uncomfortable feeling that the characters on the stage are not the only persons under investigation. The Inspector's pursuit of the truth is so intense that each member of the audience or reader of the play may wonder how he or she would fare under similar circumstances. The faults of the characters may not be ours, but they arise from the common human sins of greed, pride, selfishness and lack of self-control which we can recognize in ourselves.

The characters voice the sort of excuses that any of us might make. Gerald says, 'After all, y'know, we're respectable citizens and not criminals.' To this the Inspector replies, 'Sometimes there isn't as much difference as you think. Often, if it was left to me, I wouldn't know where to draw the line' (p. 179). The belief that being respectable means nothing more than not committing a crime is shown to be inadequate. None of the characters (except Eric when he steals) has committed any crime at all, but the damage they have done is enormous. Mr Birling feels that his public position should be enough to guarantee his respectability, but the Inspector tells him, 'Public men, Mr Birling, have responsibilities as well as privileges' (p. 195). Mrs Birling at the beginning of Act Two makes it clear that she feels herself to be socially superior to the Inspector, and she remarks contemptuously that they could not be expected to understand why the girl committed suicide, since 'Girls of that class . . .' (p. 186). She is interrupted by Sheila before she can complete the sentence, but she obviously means that the feelings of lower-class girls could not be understood by persons of her standing.

Sheila makes no such attempt to avoid the blame, acknowledging the Inspector's accusation that she has used her power as a good customer and the daughter of a well-known man to punish the girl who had offended her. But she comments, '. . . it didn't seem to be anything very terrible at the time' (p. 181). When she adds that she wishes she could help the girl now, the Inspector bluntly tells her, 'It's too late. She's dead.' Her father is equally crushed when, in Act Three, he wishes money could now help: 'I'd give thousands – yes, thousands –'. The harsh reply is, 'You're offering the money at the wrong time, Mr Birling' (p. 207).

In these various attitudes, J. B. Priestley draws attention to the common human reactions and excuses we put forward when made aware of our treatment of our fellow men – claims to respectability, public reputation, social position, unawareness of the consequences and the cry, when it is too late, of 'I would give anything to change matters.' The author is challenging us to reject these excuses and think how we personally may be responsible for the tragedy of others.

There is a further dimension to J. B. Priestley's challenge. He was writing at a time when the country was emerging from six years of war. People were intent on post-war reconstruction and many were thinking of the kind of society they should try to build. The play raises precisely this question. Was the tragedy of Eva Smith attributable to the kind of society she lived in – a society that gave most honour and reward to a man like Birling, a society where the rich exploited the poor or used them for their pleasure and where even charity depended on the whim of a person like Mrs Birling? The Inspector drives home his lesson just before he leaves: 'We don't live alone. We are members of one body. We are responsible for each other' (p. 207). In Act Two he made a chilling remark on the human need for interdependence. Speaking to Sheila and Gerald he said, 'You see, we have to share something. If there's nothing else, we'll have to share our guilt' (p. 184). J. B. Priestley's urgent plea is that in our society we find something else to share – sympathy, understanding and social responsibility.

BIRLING'S SPEECH ON THE FUTURE

The climax of the dinner party in Act One is the long speech of Mr Birling in which he surveys the future as he imagines it will develop during the married life of Sheila and Gerald (pp. 165–6). He speaks 'as a hard-headed business man', acknowledging the 'wild talk' about possible labour troubles but believing that the worst is past and a bright future is in store for Capitalism. As for war, material progress is making it impossible, and in twenty or thirty years' time, he tells the young couple, '. . . you'll be living in a world that'll have forgotten all these Capital versus Labour agitations and all these silly little war scares'.

The speech is the centre-piece of the first part of the act, and it is therefore worth considering why J. B. Priestley gave it such prominence. Since he was writing more than thirty years after the time of the play, it was not difficult for him to be wise after the event and make Birling look foolish by his over-optimistic forecast of a bright future for the world. The reference to the *Titanic* – 'unsinkable, absolutely unsinkable' – gains an easy effect since everyone knows of its loss on its maiden voyage, and Mr Birling's sneer that Russia, of course, would always be behind every other country would sound odious in the ears of a post-war audience who knew of the recent victories of the Russian forces over Hitler. We may feel, therefore, that J. B. Priestley was able perhaps too easily to gain an effect of dramatic irony (i.e. a situation where the audience possesses knowledge that a character lacks).

Even so, the speech does serve various dramatic purposes. It paints a picture of a world safe for Capitalism, a world in which bosses such as Mr Birling will thrive and threats from the working class (which Eva Smith belonged to) will have no impact. The socialism preached by 'these Bernard Shaws and H. G. Wellses' is to be countered by the practical business men having their say – and it is very clear that an expansion of material prosperity for Mr Birling's class, with little regard for others, is what he looks forward to. The action of the play will shake this attitude to its foundations. At the start, Birling is confident that he was perfectly justified in sacking a troublesome worker: towards the end he says he would give thousands to have acted differently – though fear for his own reputation contributes to this feeling.

The speech also shows a man confident in his own judgement and totally self-satisfied. Yet the audience knows that within two years Europe will be in flames and the old certainties will be gone for ever. Mr Birling's opinion is valueless. He is riding for a fall, and an hour or so later his pride will be humbled within the walls of his own house.

Mr Birling's pronouncements therefore serve a double purpose. They display him as a self-opinionated materialist whose confidence in his own judgement is a sham. Knowing, as we do, that his forecast of the future is quite wrong, we are prepared for all the certainties of his family life to be shaken also – though at this point in the play we do not know how this will come about. Secondly, the speech gives a view of society as Mr Birling and those like him see it – materialistic, enjoying 'peace and prosperity and rapid progress' with the interests of Capital 'properly protected'. He adds a postscript when, a little later, he gives 'fatherly' advice to Gerald and Eric: cranks talk about 'community and all that nonsense. But take my word for it . . . that a man has to mind his own business and look after himself and his own – and –' . . . At this point an Inspector calls.

Glossary

Alderman: formerly an elected senior official in a town or county council

Assertive: drawing attention to one's own views

Balkans: countries of S.E. Europe

Bernard Shaw: (1856–1950) famous playwright and socialist writer

Bluffed: misled, fooled

Capital: the means of production, under private control

Cranks: mentally unbalanced people holding foolish opinions

Dandy: man who is showy and affected in his dress

Dingy: dull, shabby

Disconcerting: disturbing, upsetting

Dissent: disagreement

Dumbfounded: astonished, confused

Exasperating: very irritating

Give ... rope: allow scope or opportunity

Guffaw: noisy laugh

Hard-headed: shrewd, coldly calculating

H. G. Wells: (1866–1946) influential writer of science-fiction and sociological novels

Hoax: practical joke

Hysterical: emotionally uncontrolled

Idiocies: stupidities

Impertinent: impudent, rude

Infirmary: hospital

Interpose: place between

Irony: using words to convey the opposite of their apparent meaning

Justified: can be shown to have acted rightly

Kaiser: German Emperor

Labour: the workers employed to produce goods

Moonshine: fantasy, imagination

Morbid: diseased

Music hall: theatre for light entertainment

Portentous: impressive

Potty: (slang) silly

Prejudiced: holding an opinion not based on reason or justice

Public man: one holding an official position in the community

Sardonically: bitterly and sneeringly

Scaremonger: one who spreads alarm

Scruples: doubts over what is right and wrong

Sell: (slang) confidence trick

Shilling: five pence

Sots: drunkards

Speculatively: thoughtfully forming ideas

Squiffy: (slang) slightly drunk

Steady the Buffs: take care (from an order given to the Buffs, a regiment of the British Army)

Take offence: be made upset or angry

Tantalus: a stand with a locking device for three decanters

Titanic: British liner that sank on its maiden voyage in 1912

Twenty-two and six: one pound and twelve and a half pence

Varsity: (slang) university

Vindictive: spiteful, vengeful

Warrant: official document authorizing arrest etc.

Women of the town: prostitutes

Womanizer: man who pursues women

Discussion Topics and Examination Questions

DISCUSSION TOPICS

Your understanding and appreciation of the play will be much increased if you discuss aspects of it with other people. Here are some topics you could consider:

1. How far was Eva Smith responsible for her own tragedy?
2. Discuss what you think would happen when the real inspector called after the play has ended.
3. What qualities make this play different from an ordinary thriller?
4. Since the play is continuous, what dramatic purpose is served by lowering the curtain at the end of each act?
5. It is hard to believe that in real life every single member of one family would have been involved with Eva Smith. Defend or support J. B. Priestley in the face of the criticism that he pushes coincidence too far in this play.
6. 'Why – you fool – *he knows*. Of course he knows.' Consider each character in turn and discuss how much, in your opinion, the Inspector actually does know about them at the start and how much they themselves add to his knowledge.
7. How much would you blame their parents for the actions of Sheila and Eric? How far do you think they are personally responsible?
8. Why do you feel Gerald sides with Mr and Mrs Birling at the end of the play, even though he is a member of the younger generation and hopes to be engaged to Sheila?
9. 'Pride goes before a fall.' Find evidence of this in the play and discuss the dramatic effect of the examples you choose.
10. How far do you feel the organization of society of that time was responsible for Eva Smith's tragedy?

11. The play was written about forty years ago. Is its message still relevant today?
12. Do you agree with the Inspector that 'We are responsible for each other' (p. 207)?
13. What do you think the Inspector had in mind when he gave his final warning, 'And I tell you that the time will soon come when, if men will not learn that lesson, then they will be taught it in fire and blood and anguish' (p. 207)? Has the prophecy in any way been fulfilled?
14. How practical is it in the modern world to live up to the ideal of regarding all human beings as 'members of one body'?

THE GCSE EXAMINATION

If you are studying for the GCSE examination you may find that the set texts have been selected by your teacher from a very wide list of suggestions in the examination syllabus. The questions in the examination paper will therefore be applicable to many different books. Here are some possible questions which you could answer by making use of *An Inspector Calls*:

1. Have you read a play or story in which a stranger makes a great difference to the lives of the other characters? Describe how he or she does this and with what effects.
2. Many books and plays deal with discord within a family. Show how this comes about in the text of your choice and discuss how far the discord is resolved by the end of the story.
3. Drama is often created by a conflict of attitudes between young people and their elders. Briefly describe such a situation in your chosen text and attempt to defend in turn the attitudes of (a) the young and (b) the old.
4. In some works the characters go through a process of learning about themselves. Select two contrasting characters from a book or play you know and show how each responds to this learning process.
5. Show how the emotion of fear influences the actions of two characters in a play you know and with what result.

6. Choose a text where the element of mystery is important. Show the part it plays in the story and discuss how successful the author is in creating it.

7. Many books and plays purposely leave the ending uncertain. Write about a text where this would apply, explaining why in this particular case you find such an ending satisfactory or not.

EXAMINATION QUESTIONS

1. Select *one* of the characters at the dinner party and describe in detail how that person contributed to the girl's suicide. How does that character react to the discovery that the Inspector may not be genuine?

(South Western Examinations Board C S E, 1985)

2. By referring closely to the text, describe Arthur Birling's part in the play. What are the main features of his character?

(South Western Examinations Board C S E, 1985)

3. Sheila says, 'We must stop all these silly pretences.' Give *three* pretences exposed by the Inspector and explain in detail what they tell us about the attitudes of the people involved.

(South Western Examinations Board C S E, 1984)

4. Describe in detail what happens after the Inspector's departure until the end of the play. How does this scene illustrate Priestley's ability to produce dramatic suspense?

(South Western Examinations Board C S E, 1984)

5. Imagine that you are in charge of a production of *An Inspector Calls*. Explain how you would handle the presentation and portrayal of the Inspector.

(Associated Examining Board, 1981)

6. *An Inspector Calls* was first performed in 1945. Giving your reasons, show whether you think the play's social criticism is dated or whether you think it is just as relevant today.

(Welsh Joint Education Committee, 1983)

7. Write an introduction to the play such as might be suitable for a theatre programme, mentioning the following: the kind of play it is; its themes and ideas; the main characters and situations; the setting and background. Generally prepare the audience for the first scene, without spoiling it by giving away the plot.

(Welsh Joint Education Committee, 1983)